THE NATURE OF
TEXAS

An Introduction to Familiar Plants, Animals & Natural Attractions

By James Kavanagh

Illustrations by Raymond Leung
Introduction by James C. Rettie

WATERFORD PRESS

Publisher's Cataloging in Publication Data
Kavanagh, James Daniel, 1960 -
The Nature of Texas. An Introduction to Familiar Plants, Animals & Natural Attractions. Includes biographical references and index.
1. Natural History – Texas. 2. Animals – Identification – Texas.
3. Plants – Identification – Texas. 4. Tourism – Texas.

Library of Congress Catalog Card Number: 2020932821
ISBN: 978-1-62005-375-1

The introductory essay, "BUT A WATCH IN THE NIGHT" by JAMES C. RETTIE is from FOREVER THE LAND by RUSSELL AND KATE LORD. Copyright © 1950 by Harper & Brothers, copyright renewed © 1978 by Russell and Kate Lord. Reprinted with permission of HarperCollins Publishers.

The maps in this guide are adapted from maps copyright © by the United States Geological Survey, © The National Atlas of the United States and are reproduced with permission.

Waterford Press' toll-free order/information line is (800) 434-2555.
Download product information from our website: www.waterfordpress.com

While every attempt has been made to ensure the accuracy of the information in this guide, it is important to note that experts often disagree with one another regarding the common name, size, appearance, habitat, distribution and taxonomy of species. For permissions, or to share comments, e-mail editor@waterfordpress.com.

CONTENTS

To our friend and colleague,

Raymond Leung

The Nature of Texas is intended to provide novice naturalists with a pocket reference to the state's familiar and distinctive species of plants and animals and the outstanding natural attractions found in Texas.

The guide's primary purpose is to introduce the reader to common plants and animals and to highlight the diversity of species found in Texas. Its secondary purpose is to show how all species in each ecosystem found here – from swamps to montane forests – depend on each other, directly and indirectly, for survival.

Environmental education begins when people learn to appreciate the plants and animals in their immediate environment. When they start to care about local species – which often begins by learning their names – they take the first step toward learning about, and understanding their place, as an animal, within an ecosystem.

The guide opens with a brief introduction to evolution. This is not intended in any way to dispute creationism, but is merely intended to illustrate the similarities and differences between major groups of plants and animals and show when each appeared in geologic time. To study the fossil record is fascinating in and of itself, but one of the most stunning things it reveals is a number of transitional species that are intermediary between different classes of organisms.

The brilliant introductory essay by James C. Rettie provides a simplified view of the evolution of life on earth, and the role that man – the animal – has played to date.

J.D.K.

BUT A WATCH IN THE NIGHT

BY JAMES C. RETTIE

James C. Rettie wrote the following essay while working for the National Forest Service in 1948. In a flash of brilliance, he converted the statistics from an existing government pamphlet on soil erosion into an analogy for the ages.

OUT BEYOND OUR SOLAR SYSTEM there is a planet called Copernicus. It came into existence some four or five billion years before the birth of our earth. In due course of time it became inhabited by a race of intelligent men.

About 750 million years ago the Copernicans had developed the motion picture machine to a point well in advance of the stage that we have reached. Most of the cameras that we now use in motion picture work are geared to take twenty-four pictures per second on a continuous strip of film. When such film is run through a projector, it throws a series of images on the screen and these change with a rapidity that gives the visual impression of normal movement. If a motion is too swift for the human eye to see it in detail, it can be captured and artificially slowed down by means of the slow-motion camera. This one is geared to take many more shots per second – ninety-six or even more than that. When the slow motion film is projected at the normal speed of twenty-four pictures per second, we can see just how the jumping horse goes over a hurdle.

What about motion that is too slow to be seen by the human eye? That problem has been solved by the use of the time-lapse camera. In this one, the shutter is geared to take only one shot per second, or one per minute, or even one per hour – depending upon the kind of movement that is being photographed. When the time-lapse film is projected at the normal speed of twenty-four pictures per second, it is possible to see a bean sprout growing up out of the ground. Time-lapse films are useful in the study of many types of motion too slow to be observed by the unaided, human eye.

The Copernicans, it seems, had time-lapse cameras some 757 million years ago and they also had superpowered telescopes that gave them a clear view of what was happening upon this earth. They decided to make a film record of the life history of earth and to make it on the scale of one picture per year. The photography has been in progress during the last 757 million years.

In the near future, a Copernican interstellar expedition will arrive upon our earth and bring with it a copy of the time-lapse film. Arrangements will be made for showing the entire film in one continuous run. This will begin at midnight of New Year's eve and continue day and night without a single stop until midnight on December 31. The rate of projection will be 24 pictures per second. Time on the screen will thus seem to move at the rate of twenty-four years per second; 1440 years per minute; 86,400 years per hour; approximately two million years per day and sixty-two million years per month. The normal lifespan of individual man will occupy about three seconds. The full period of earth history that will be unfolded on the screen (some 757 million years) will extend from what the geologists call the Pre-Cambrian times up to the present. This will, by no means, cover the full time-span of the earth's geological history but it will embrace the period since the advent of living organisms.

During the months of January, February, and March the picture will be desolate and dreary. The shape of the land masses and the oceans will bear little or no resemblance to those that we know. The violence of geological erosion will be much in evidence. Rains will pour down on the land and promptly go booming down to the seas. There will be no clear streams anywhere except where the rains fall upon hard rock. Everywhere on the steeper ground the stream channels will be filled with boulders hurled down by rushing waters. Raging torrents and dry stream beds will keep alternating in quick succession. High mountains will seem to melt like so much butter in the sun. The shifting of land into the seas, later to be thrust up as new mountains, will be going on at a grand scale.

Early in April there will be some indication of the presence of single-celled living organisms in some of the warmer and sheltered coastal waters. By the end of the month it will be noticed that some of these organisms have become multicellular. A few of them, including the Trilobites, will be encased in hard shells.

Toward the end of May, the first vertebrates will appear, but they will still be aquatic creatures. In June about 60 percent of the land area that we know as North America will be under water. One broad channel will occupy the space where the Rocky Mountains now stand. Great deposits of limestone will be forming under some of the shallower seas. Oil and gas deposits will be in process of formation – also under shallow seas. On land there will be no sign of vegetation. Erosion will be rampant, tearing loose particles and chunks of rock and grinding them into sand and silt to be spewed out by the streams into bays and estuaries.

About the middle of July the first land plants will appear and take up the tremendous job of soil building. Slowly, very slowly, the mat of vegetation will spread, always battling for its life against the power of erosion. Almost foot by foot, the plant life will advance, lacing down with its root structures whatever pulverized rock material it can find. Leaves and stems will be giving added protection against the loss of the soil foothold. The increasing vegetation will pave the way for the land animals that will live upon it.

Early in August the seas will be teeming with fish. This will be what geologists call the Devonian period. Some of the races of these fish will be breathing by means of lung tissue instead of through gill tissues. Before the month is over, some of the lung fish will go ashore and take on a crude lizard-like appearance. Here are the first amphibians.

In early September the insects will put in their appearance. Some will look like huge dragonflies and will have a wing span of 24 inches. Large portions of the land masses will now be covered with heavy vegetation that will include the primitive spore-propagating trees. Layer upon layer of this plant growth will build up, later to appear as coal deposits. About the middle of this month, there will be evidence of the first seed-bearing plants and the first reptiles. Heretofore, the land animals will have been amphibians that could reproduce their kind only by depositing a soft egg mass in quiet waters. The reptiles will be shown to be freed from the aquatic bond because they can reproduce by means of a shelled egg in which the embryo and its nurturing liquids are sealed and thus protected from destructive evaporation. Before September is over, the first dinosaurs will be seen – creatures destined to dominate the animal realm for about 140 million years and then to disappear.

In October there will be series of mountain uplifts along what is now the eastern coast of the United States. A creature with feathered limbs – half bird and half reptile in appearance – will take itself into the air. Some small and rather unpretentious animals will be seen to bring forth their young in a form that is a miniature replica of the parents and to feed these young on milk secreted by mammary glands in the female parent. The emergence of this mammalian form of animal life will be recognized as one of the great events in geologic time. October will also witness the high-water mark of the dinosaurs – creatures ranging in size from that of the modern goat to monsters like Brontosaurus that weighed some 40 tons. Most of them will be placid vegetarians, but a few will be hideous-looking carnivores, like Allosaurus and Tyrannosaurus. Some of the herbivorous dinosaurs will be clad in bony armor for protection against their flesh-eating comrades.

November will bring pictures of a sea extending from the Gulf of Mexico to the Arctic in space now occupied by the Rocky Mountains. A few of the reptiles will take to the air on bat-like wings. One of these, called Pteranodon, will have a wingspread of 15 feet. There will be a rapid development of the modern flowering plants, modern trees, and modern insects. The dinosaurs will disappear. Toward the end of the month there will be a tremendous land disturbance in which the Rocky Mountains will rise out of the sea to assume a dominating place in the North American landscape.

As the picture runs on into December it will show the mammals in command of the animal life. Seed-bearing trees and grasses will have covered most of the land with a heavy mantle of vegetation. Only the areas newly thrust up from the sea will be barren. Most of the streams will be crystal clear. The turmoil of geological erosion will be confined to localized areas. About December 25 will begin the cutting of the Grand Canyon of the Colorado River. Grinding down through layer after layer of sedimentary strata, this stream will finally expose deposits laid down in Pre-Cambrian times. Thus in the walls of that canyon will appear geological formations dating from recent times to the period when the earth had no living organisms upon it.

The picture will run on through the latter days of December and even up to its final day with still no sign of mankind. The spectators will become alarmed in the fear that man has somehow been left out. But not so; sometime about noon on December 31 (one million years ago) will appear a stooped, massive creature of man-like proportions. This will be Pithecanthropus, the Java ape man. For tools and weapons he will have nothing but crude stone and wooden clubs. His children will live a precarious existence threatened on the one side by hostile animals and on the other by tremendous climatic changes. Ice sheets – in places 4,000 feet deep – will form in the northern parts of North America and Eurasia. Four times this glacial ice will push southward to cover half the continents. With each advance the plant and animal life will be swept under or pushed southward. With each recession of the ice, life will struggle to re-establish itself in the wake of the retreating glaciers. The woolly mammoth, the musk ox, and the caribou all will fight to maintain themselves near the ice line. Sometimes they will be caught and put into cold storage – skin, flesh, blood, bones, and all.

The picture will run on through supper time with still very little evidence of man's presence on earth. It will be about 11 o'clock when Neanderthal man appears. Another half hour will go by before the appearance of Cro-Magnon man living in caves and painting crude animal pictures on the walls of his dwelling. Fifteen minutes more will bring Neolithic man, knowing how to chip stone and thus produce sharp cutting edges for spears and tools. In a few minutes more it will appear that man has domesticated the dog, the sheep and, possibly, other animals. He will then begin the use of milk. He will also learn the arts of basket weaving and the making of pottery and dugout canoes.

The dawn of civilization will not come until about five or six minutes before the end of the picture. The story of the Egyptians, the Babylonians, the Greeks, and the Romans will unroll during the fourth, the third, and the second minute before the end. At 58 minutes and 43 seconds past 11:00 P.M. (just 1 minute and 17 seconds before the end) will come the beginning of the Christian era. Columbus will discover the new world 20 seconds before the end.

The Declaration of Independence will be signed just 7 seconds before the final curtain comes down.

In those few moments of geologic time will be the story of all that has happened since we became a nation. And what a story it will be! A human swarm will sweep across the face of the continent and take it away from the [Native Americans]. They will change it far more radically than it has ever been changed before in a comparable time. The great virgin forests will be seen going down before ax and fire. The soil, covered for eons by its protective mantle of trees and grasses, will be laid bare to the ravages of water and wind erosion. Streams that had been flowing clear will, once again, take up a load of silt and push it toward the seas. Humus and mineral salts, both vital elements of productive soil, will be seen to vanish at a terrifying rate.

The railroads and highways and cities that will spring up may divert attention, but they cannot cover up the blight of man's recent activities. In great sections of Asia, it will be seen that man must utilize cow dung and every scrap of available straw or grass for fuel to cook his food. The forests that once provided wood for this purpose will be gone without a trace. The use of these agricultural wastes for fuel, in place of returning them to the land, will be leading to increasing soil impoverishment. Here and there will be seen a dust storm darkening the landscape over an area a thousand miles across. Man-creatures will be shown counting their wealth in terms of bits of printed paper representing other bits of a scarce but comparatively useless yellow metal that is kept buried in strong vaults. Meanwhile, the soil, the only real wealth that can keep mankind alive on the face of this earth is savagely being cut loose from its ancient moorings and washed into the seven seas.

We have just arrived upon this earth. How long will we stay?

Because this guide has been written for the novice, every attempt has been made to simplify presentation of the material. Illustrations are accompanied by brief descriptions of key features, and technical terms have been held to a minimum. Plants and animals are arranged more-or-less in their taxonomic groupings. Exceptions have been made when nontraditional groupings facilitate field identification for the novice (e.g., wildflowers are grouped by color).

ILLUSTRATIONS

The majority of animal illustrations show the adult male in its breeding coloration. Plant illustrations are designed to highlight the characteristics that are most conspicuous in the field. It is important to note that illustrations are merely meant as guidelines; coloration, size and shape will vary depending on age, sex or season.

SPECIES CHECKLISTS

The species checklists at the back of this book are provided to allow you to keep track of the plants and animals you identify.

TIPS ON FIELD IDENTIFICATION

Identifying a species in the field can be as simple as one, two, three:

1. Note key markings, characteristics and/or behaviors;
2. Find an illustration that matches; and
3. Read the text to confirm your sighting.

Identifying mammals or birds in the field is not fundamentally different than identifying trees, flowers or other forms of life. It is simply a matter of knowing what to look for. Reading the introductory text to each section will make you aware of key characteristics of each group and allow you to use the guide more effectively in the field.

N.B. – We refer primarily to familiar species in this guide and do not list all species within any group. References listed in the bibliography at the back of this guide provide more detailed information about specific areas of study.

SPECIES DESCRIPTION

The species descriptions have been fragmented to simplify presentation of information:

① RUBY-THROATED HUMMINGBIRD
② *Selasphorus platycercus*

③ **Size:** 4–5 in. (10–13 cm)

④ **Description:** Small, iridescent green bird has a rose red throat and a broad tail. Note white line under its bill.

⑤ **Habitat:** Meadows, grasslands from the plains to the timberline.

⑥ **Comments:** Wings produce a cricket-like trilling sound in flight.

① COMMON NAME

The name in bold type indicates the common name of the species. It is important to note that a single species may have many common names.

② *Scientific Name*

The italicized Latin words refer to an organism's scientific name, a universally accepted two-part term that precisely defines its relationship to other organisms. The first capitalized word, the genus, refers to groups of closely related organisms. The second term, the species name, refers to organisms that look similar and interbreed freely. If the second word in the term is 'spp.', this indicates there are several species in the genus that look similar to the one illustrated. If a third word appears in the term, it identifies a subspecies, a group of individuals that are even more closely related.

③ Size

Generally indicates the maximum length of animals (nose to tail tip) and the maximum height of plants. Butterfly and moth measurements refer to wingspan. Exceptions are noted in the text.

④ Description

Refers to key markings and/or characteristics that help to distinguish a species.

⑤ Habitat

Where a species lives/can be found.

⑥ Comments

General information regarding distinctive behaviors, diet, vocalizations, related species, etc.

EVOLUTION OF ANIMALS

Animals are living organisms that can generally be distinguished from plants in four ways:

1. They feed on plants and other animals;
2. They have a nervous system;
3. They can move freely and are not rooted; and
4. Their cells do not have rigid walls or contain chlorophyll.

All animals are members of the animal kingdom, a group consisting of more than a million species. Species are classified within the animal kingdom according to their evolutionary relationships to one another.

Most of the animals discussed in this guide are members of the group called vertebrates. They all possess backbones and most have complex brains and highly developed senses.

The earliest vertebrates appeared in the oceans about 500 million years ago. Today, surviving species are divided into five main groups:

1. Fishes
2. Amphibians
3. Reptiles
4. Birds
5. Mammals

Following is a simplified description of the evolution of the vertebrates and the differences between groups.

FISHES

The oldest form of vertebrate life, fishes evolved from invertebrate sea creatures 400–500 million years ago. All are cold-blooded (ectothermic) and their activity levels are largely influenced by the surrounding environment.

The first species were armored and jawless and fed by filtering tiny organisms from water and mud. Surviving members of this group include lampreys and hagfishes. Jawless fishes were succeeded by jawed fishes that quickly came to dominate the seas, and still do today. The major surviving groups include:

1. **Sharks and rays** – more primitive species that possess soft skeletons made of cartilage; and
2. **Bony fishes** – a more advanced group of fishes that have bony skeletons, it includes most of the fishes currently existing.

Shark

Ray

Bony Fish

Physiological Characteristics of Fishes

- **Heart and gills**
  A two-chambered heart circulates the blood through a simple system of arteries and veins. Gills act like lungs and allow fishes to absorb dissolved oxygen from the water into their bloodstream.

- **Nervous system**
  Small anterior brain is connected to a spinal cord which runs the length of the body.

- **Digestive system**
  Digestive system is complete. A number of specialized organs produce enzymes that help to break down food in the stomach and intestines. Kidneys extract urine from the blood and waste is eliminated through the anus.

- **Reproduction**
  In most fishes, the female lays numerous eggs in water and the male fertilizes them externally. Young usually hatch as larvae, and the larval period ranges from a few hours to several years. Survival rate of young is low.

- **Senses**
  Most have the senses of taste, touch, smell, hearing and sight, although their vision is generally poor. Fishes hear and feel by sensing vibrations and temperature and pressure changes in the surrounding water.

AMPHIBIANS

The first limbed land-dwellers, amphibians evolved from fishes 300–400 million years ago and became the dominant land vertebrates for more than 100 million years. Like fishes, amphibians are cold-blooded and their activity levels are largely influenced by the environment.

The first fish-like amphibian ancestors to escape the water were those that had the ability to breathe air and possessed strong, paired fins that allowed them to wriggle onto mud-flats and sandbars. (Living relics of this group include five species of lungfish and the rare coelacanth.) Although amphibians were able to exploit rich new habitats on land, they remained largely dependent on aquatic environments for survival and reproduction.

The major surviving groups are:

1. **Salamanders** – slender-bodied, short-legged, long-tailed creatures that live secretive lives in dark, damp areas; and
2. **Frogs and toads** – squat-bodied animals with long hind legs, large heads and large eyes. Frogs are smooth skinned, toads have warty skin.

Salamander

Frog

Toad

Advances Made Over Fishes

- **Lungs and legs**
  By developing lungs and legs, amphibians freed themselves from the competition for food in aquatic environments and were able to flourish on land.

- **Improved circulatory system**
  Amphibians evolved a heart with three chambers that enhanced gas exchange in the lungs and provided body tissues with highly oxygenated blood.

- **Ears**
  Frogs and toads developed external ears that enhanced their hearing ability, an essential adaptation for surviving on land.

- **Reproduction**
  Most amphibians reproduced like fish. Salamanders differ in that most fertilize eggs internally rather than externally. In many, the male produced a sperm packet, which the female collected and used to fertilize eggs as they were laid.

REPTILES

Reptiles appeared 300–350 million years ago. They soon came to dominate the earth, and continued to rule the land, sea and air for more than 130 million years. Cold-blooded like amphibians, reptiles evolved a host of characteristics that made them better suited for life on land.

About 65 million years ago, the dominant reptiles mysteriously underwent a mass extinction. A popular theory suggests this was caused by a giant meteor hitting the earth, which sent up a huge dust cloud that blotted out the sun. The lack of sun and subsequently low temperatures caused many plants and animals to perish.

The major surviving reptilian groups are:

1. **Turtles** – hard-shelled reptiles with short legs;
2. **Lizards** – scaly-skinned reptiles with long legs and tails;
3. **Snakes** – long, legless reptiles with scaly skin; and
4. **Crocodilians** – very large reptiles with elongated snouts, toothy jaws and long tails.

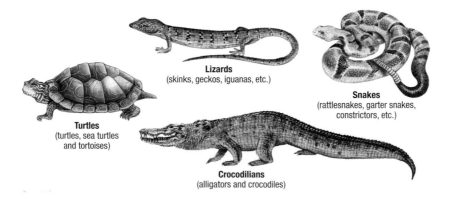

Lizards
(skinks, geckos, iguanas, etc.)

Snakes
(rattlesnakes, garter snakes, constrictors, etc.)

Turtles
(turtles, sea turtles and tortoises)

Crocodilians
(alligators and crocodiles)

Advances Made Over Amphibians

- **Dry, scaly skin**
  Their dry skin prevents water loss and also protects them from predators.

- **Posture**
  Many reptiles evolved an upright posture and strong legs, which enhanced their mobility on land.

- **Improved heart and lungs**
  Their heart and lungs were more efficient, which heightened their activity levels. The heart had four chambers – although the division between ventricles was usually incomplete – making it less likely that oxygenated and deoxygenated blood would mix.

- **Defense**
  They were agile and better able to defend themselves, having sharp claws and teeth or beaks capable of inflicting wounds.

BIRDS

Birds evolved from reptiles 100–200 million years ago. Unlike species before them, birds were warm-blooded (endothermic) and able to regulate their body temperature internally.* This meant that they could maintain high activity levels despite fluctuations in environmental temperature. They are believed to have evolved from a group of gliding reptiles, with their scaly legs considered proof of their reptilian heritage.

Birds come in a vast array of groups. All have feathered bodies, beaks, lack teeth and have forelimbs modified into wings. Most can fly.

Advances Made Over Reptiles

- **Ability to fly**
  By evolving flight, birds were able to exploit environments that were inaccessible to their competitors and predators. The characteristics they evolved that allowed them to fly included wings, feathers, hollow bones and an enhanced breathing capacity.

- **Warm-blooded**
  An insulating layer of feathers enhanced their capacity to retain heat. They also had true four-chambered hearts that enhanced their ability to maintain high activity levels in varying environments.

- **Keen senses**
  Birds evolved very keen senses of vision and hearing and developed complex behavioral and communicative patterns.

- **Reproduction**
  Fertilization was internal and the eggs had hard, rather than leathery, shells. Unlike most reptiles, birds incubated their eggs themselves and protected and nurtured their young for a period of time following birth.

* There is still a debate over whether or not some dinosaurs were warm-blooded.

MAMMALS

Mammals evolved from reptiles 100–200 million years ago. Though warm-blooded like birds, they are believed to have different reptilian ancestors. In addition to being warm-blooded, mammals also evolved physiological adaptations that allowed them to hunt prey and avoid predation better than their competitors.

Mammals quickly exploited the habitats left vacant by the dinosaurs and have been the dominant land vertebrates for the past 65 million years. Man is a relatively new addition to the group, having a lineage of less than 3 million years.

Mammals have evolved into three distinct groups, all of which have living representatives:

1. **Monotremes** – egg-laying mammals;
2. **Marsupials** – pouched mammals that bear living, embryonic young; and
3. **Placentals** – mammals that bear fully-developed young.

Monotremes
(platypus and echidna)

Marsupials
(opossums, kangaroos etc.)

Placentals
(squirrels, humans, dogs, rats etc.)

Advances Made Over Birds

- **Reproduction**
  Fertilization was internal, but in most, the young developed in the female's uterus instead of an egg. After birth, the young were fed and nurtured by adults for an extensive period, during which they learned behavioral lessons from their elders and siblings. This emphasis on learned responses at an early age is believed to have contributed to the superior intelligence and reproductive success of the group.

- **Hearing**
  Most had three bones in the middle ear to enhance hearing. (Birds and reptiles have one.)

- **Teeth**
  Many developed specialized teeth that allowed them to rely on a variety of food sources. Incisors were for cutting, canines for tearing and molars for chewing or shearing.

- **Breathing**
  Mammals evolved a diaphragm, which increased breathing efficiency.

- **Posture**
  Many evolved long, strong legs and were very agile on land.

EVOLUTION OF PLANTS

Plants are living organisms that can generally be distinguished from animals in four ways:

1. They synthesize their own food needed for maintenance and growth from carbon dioxide, water and sunlight;
2. They do not have a nervous system;
3. Most are rooted and cannot move around easily; and
4. Their cells have rigid walls and contain chlorophyll, a pigment needed for photosynthesis.

All plants are members of the plant kingdom. According to the fossil record, plants evolved from algae that originated nearly 3 billion years ago. Since then, plants have evolved into millions of species in a mind-boggling assortment of groups.

Most North American plants are classified into two main groups:

1. **Gymnosperms** – plants with naked seeds; and
2. **Angiosperms** – flowering plants with enclosed seeds.

Gymnosperms   Angiosperms

GYMNOSPERMS – THE NAKED SEED PLANTS

This group of mostly evergreen trees and shrubs includes some of the largest and oldest known plants. They began to appear around 300–400 million years ago, and were the dominant plant species on earth for nearly 200 million years. The most successful surviving group of gymnosperms are the conifers, which include such species as pines, spruces, firs, larches and junipers.

Most conifers are evergreen and have small needle-like or scale-like leaves that are adapted to withstand extreme temperature changes. Some species are deciduous, but most retain their leaves for two or more years before shedding them.

Reproduction

Most conifers produce cones – wood-like fruits that contain the male and female gametes. The male cones produce pollen that is carried by the wind to settle between the scales of female cones on other trees. The pollen stimulates ovules to change into seeds, and the scales of the female cone close up to protect the seeds. When the seeds are ripe, up to two years later, environmental conditions stimulate the cone to open its scales and the naked seeds to fall to the ground.

ANGIOSPERMS – THE FLOWERING PLANTS

Angiosperms first appeared in the fossil record around 130 million years ago. They quickly adapted to a wide variety of environments and succeeded gymnosperms as the dominant land plants. Their reproductive success was largely due to two key adaptations:

Advances Made Over Gymnosperms

1. They produced flowers that attracted pollinating agents such as insects and birds; and
2. They produced seeds encased in fruits to aid in seed dispersal.

Angiosperms are classified in two main groups:

1. **Monocots** – plants with one embryonic leaf at germination, parallel-veined leaves, stems with scattered vascular bundles with little or no cambium (group includes grasses, cattails, orchids and corn); and
2. **Dicots** – plants with two embryonic leaves at germination, net-veined leaves, stems with cylindrical vascular bundles in a regular pattern that contain cambium (group includes more than 200,000 species ranging from tiny herbs to huge trees).

Angiosperms make up a diverse and widespread group of plants ranging from trees and shrubs such as oaks, cherries, maples, hazelnuts and apples, to typical flowers like lilies, orchids, roses, daisies and violets. The trees and shrubs within this group are commonly referred to as deciduous and most shed their leaves annually.

Reproduction

A typical flower has colorful petals that encircle the male and female reproductive structures (see illustration p. 133). The male stamens are composed of thin filaments supporting anthers containing pollen. The female pistil contains unfertilized seeds in the swollen basal part called the ovary. Pollination occurs when pollen, carried by the wind or animals, reaches the pistil.

Once fertilization has occurred, the ovules develop into seeds and the ovary into a fruit. The fruit and seeds mature together, with the fruit ripening to the point where the seeds are capable of germinating. At maturity, each seed contains an embryo and a food supply to nourish it upon germination. Upon ripening, the fruit may fall to the ground with the seeds still inside, as in peaches, cherries and squash, or it may burst open and scatter its seeds in the wind, like poplar trees, willows and dandelions.

Fruit comes in many forms, from grapes, tomatoes, apples and pears, to pea and bean pods, nuts, burrs and capsules. Regardless of its shape, fruit enhances the reproductive success of angiosperms in two important ways. First, it helps to protect the seeds from the elements until they have fully matured, enabling them to survive unfavorable conditions. Second, fruit aids in seed dispersal. Some fruits are eaten by animals that eventually release the seeds in their feces, an ideal growing medium. Others may be spiny or burred so they catch on the coats of animals, or may have special features that enable them to be carried away from their parent plant by the wind or water.

GEOLOGICAL TIMESCALE

ERA	PERIOD	MYA*	EVENTS
CENOZOIC	HOLOCENE	.01	Dominance of humans.
	QUATERNARY	2.5	First human civilizations.
	TERTIARY	65	Mammals, birds, insects and angiosperms dominate the land.
MESOZOIC	CRETACEOUS	135	Dinosaurs extinct. Mammals, insects and angiosperms undergo great expansion. Gymnosperms decline.
	JURASSIC	190	Age of Reptiles; dinosaurs dominant. First birds appear.
	TRIASSIC	225	First dinosaurs and mammals appear. Gymnosperms are dominant plants.
PALEOZOIC	PERMIAN	280	Great expansion of reptiles causes amphibians to decline. Many marine invertebrates become extinct.
	CARBONIFEROUS	340	Age of Amphibians; amphibians dominant. First reptiles appear. Fish undergo a great expansion.
	DEVONIAN	400	Age of Fishes; fishes dominant. First amphibians, insects and gymnosperms appear.
	SILURIAN	430	First jawed fishes appear. Plants move onto land.
	ORDOVICIAN	500	First vertebrates appear.
	CAMBRIAN	600	Marine invertebrates and algae abundant.

*Millions of years ago

GENERALIZED RELIEF

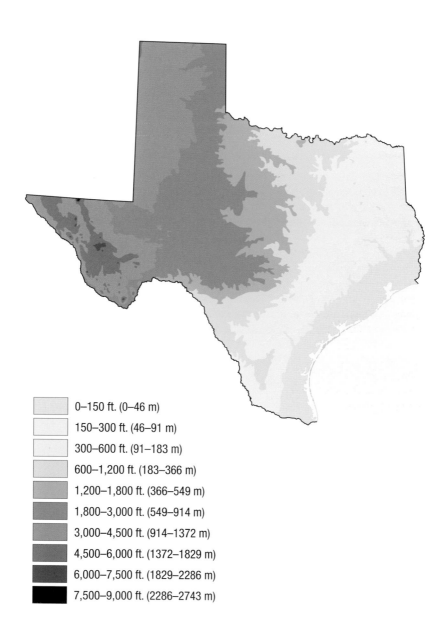

0–150 ft. (0–46 m)

150–300 ft. (46–91 m)

300–600 ft. (91–183 m)

600–1,200 ft. (183–366 m)

1,200–1,800 ft. (366–549 m)

1,800–3,000 ft. (549–914 m)

3,000–4,500 ft. (914–1372 m)

4,500–6,000 ft. (1372–1829 m)

6,000–7,500 ft. (1829–2286 m)

7,500–9,000 ft. (2286–2743 m)

GEOGRAPHY

Highest Point: 8,749 ft. (2,667 m) Guadalupe Peak

Area: 261,797 sq. mi. (678,054 sq. km)

The second largest state after Alaska, Texas is a place of remarkably varied landscapes offering features of both the humid American south and the parched southwest. Geographers divide the state into four main physical regions: Gulf Coastal Plains, Interior Lowlands, Great Plains, and Basin and Range.

NOTABLE FEATURES

Gulf Coast and Barrier Islands

The Texas Gulf Coast is punctuated with 7 major estuaries including Corpus Christi and Galveston Bay. Just offshore a series of barrier islands stretch some 300 miles along the coast. The most prominent is 130-mile long Padre Island, the longest barrier island in the world. Boasting the largest undeveloped barrier island ecosystem in North America, it includes Padre Island National Seashore.

Waterways and Playas

Texas has 15 major rivers, including the mighty Rio Grande that forms the state's border with Mexico. More than 3,700 named streams are tributaries of these river systems and many are prime angling waters. Dams have created 212 reservoirs to provide water for agriculture, ranching, and domestic use. These modern reservoirs include Caddo Lake in eastern Texas, once much smaller and the only natural lake within Texas borders. The High Plains region is dotted with more than 19,000 playas, shallow lakes that intermittently fill with seasonal rainwater. Although they do not contain water year-round, playas are vital way stations for waterfowl migrating along the Central Flyway.

Cliffs and Canyons

Several dramatic canyons plunge deep into the rolling Texas plains. Palo Duro Canyon, the second largest in the U.S. after the Grand Canyon, is 120 miles long, up to 20 miles wide, and reaches a depth of 800 feet. It and the Caprock Canyons are part of the Caprock Escarpment, a massive cliff formation that rises above a high plain encompassing more than 35,000 square miles of the Texas Panhandle. Called the Llano Estacado, meaning palisaded plain, this vast flat plateau was named by the Spanish explorer Coronado in 1541.

ECOSYSTEMS

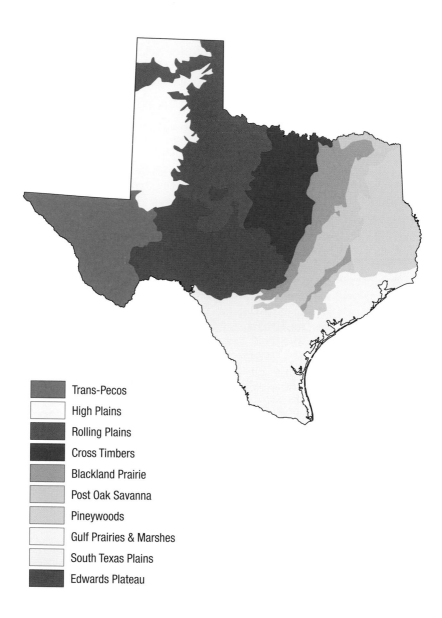

Trans-Pecos
High Plains
Rolling Plains
Cross Timbers
Blackland Prairie
Post Oak Savanna
Pineywoods
Gulf Prairies & Marshes
South Texas Plains
Edwards Plateau

ECOREGIONS

TRANS-PECOS

The Trans-Pecos is the most topographically and geologically complex region of Texas. It occupies the extreme western part of the state eastward generally to the Pecos River. This is a region of diverse habitats and vegetation, varying from the desert valleys and plateaus to wooded mountain slopes. Elevations range from less than 2,000 ft. (600 m) to more than 8,749 ft. (2,667 m) at Guadalupe Peak.

HIGH PLAINS

The High Plains region, together with the Rolling Plains comprise the southern end of the Great Plains of the central United States. The High Plains is a relatively level high plateau, separated from the Rolling Plains by the Caprock Escarpment. Elevations range from 3,000 ft. (900 m) to 4,500 ft. (1350 m) above sea level.

ROLLING PLAINS

Several Texas rivers begin in the gently rolling hills and broad flats of the Rolling Plains. These rivers and their numerous tributaries are responsible for the rolling character of the land. The rivers have cut canyons that shelter some plants and animals typical of the Rocky Mountains.

CROSS TIMBERS

Early travelers through north Texas coined the name "Cross Timbers" by their repeated crossings of these timbered areas that proved to be a barrier to their travel on the open prairies to the east and west. This area in north and central Texas includes areas with high density of trees and irregular plains and prairies. Soils are primarily sandy to loamy.

BLACKLAND PRAIRIE

The Blackland Prairie region is named for the deep, fertile black soils that characterize the area. Because of the fertile soils, much of the original prairie has been plowed to produce food and forage crops.

POST OAK SAVANNA

The Post Oak Savanna region is a transitional area for many plants and animals whose ranges extend northward into the Great Plains or eastward into the forests. Dominant vegetation is post oak and blackjack oak woodland or savanna.

PINEYWOODS

Rolling terrain covered with pines and oaks, and rich bottomlands with tall hardwoods, characterize the forests of the East Texas Pineywoods. This region is part of a much larger area of pine-hardwood forest that extends into Louisiana, Arkansas, and Oklahoma.

GULF PRAIRIES & MARSHES

This region is a nearly level, slowly drained plain less than 150 feet in elevation, dissected by streams and rivers flowing into the Gulf of Mexico. The region includes barrier islands along the coast, salt grass marshes surrounding bays and estuaries, remnant tallgrass prairies, oak parklands and oak mottes scattered along the coast, and tall woodlands in the river bottomlands.

SOUTH TEXAS PLAINS

The South Texas Brush Country, a region of level to rolling lands is characterized by thorny shrubs and trees and scattered patches of palms and subtropical woodlands in the Rio Grande Valley. Livestock grazing and deer hunting are principal land uses

EDWARDS PLATEAU

The Edwards Plateau region is characterized by spring-fed rivers and stony hills. It comprises an area of central Texas commonly known as the Texas Hill Country. It is a land of many springs, stony hills, and steep canyons. The region is home to a whole host of rare plants and animals found nowhere else on Earth.

PRECIPITATION

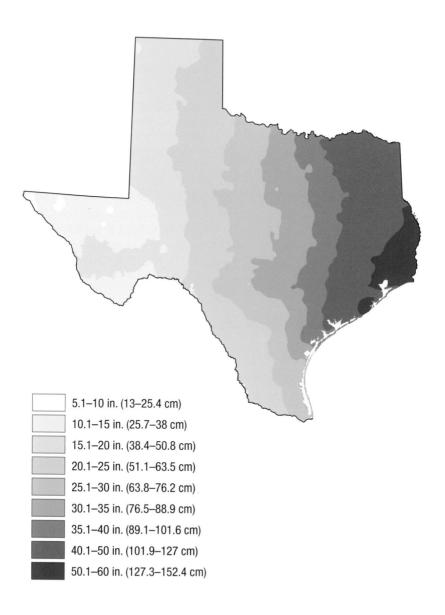

5.1–10 in. (13–25.4 cm)

10.1–15 in. (25.7–38 cm)

15.1–20 in. (38.4–50.8 cm)

20.1–25 in. (51.1–63.5 cm)

25.1–30 in. (63.8–76.2 cm)

30.1–35 in. (76.5–88.9 cm)

35.1–40 in. (89.1–101.6 cm)

40.1–50 in. (101.9–127 cm)

50.1–60 in. (127.3–152.4 cm)

CLIMATE

The geographic location of Texas is a crossroads where eastern habitats meet western ones and southern subtropical habitats meet northern temperate ones. The annual rainfall can range from eight inches in the deserts of far west Texas to 56 inches per year in the swamps of east Texas.

Three overall climate types influence the types of plant species that are common in each region. A Modified Marine climate typically brings annual rainfall of 20 to nearly 60 inches (51–150 cm) or more to the Gulf Coastal Plains, and roughly the same amount of precipitation to the Interior Lowlands. Dense forests, lush grasslands, widespread wetlands, and both freshwater and saltwater marshes of the Texas Pineywoods, Hill Country, Blackland Prairie, and southern plains reflect this ample rainfall. Much of the area experiences extremely warm, humid summers. A more moderate Continental Steppe climate prevails in the Texas High Plains and Panhandle, both extensions of the Great Plains and populated by water-sparing grasses and scrublands. An arid Mountain climate dominates southwest Texas. Typically receiving less than 12 inches of rain annually, this Trans-Pecos or Big Bend region is home to the Chihuahuan Desert and the dramatic mountains of the Guadalupe, Chisos, and Davis ranges – the southernmost extension of the Rockies.

MAMMALS

Most mammals are warm-blooded, furred creatures that have four limbs and a tail, five digits on each foot, and several different kinds of teeth. All North American species give birth to live young, which feed on milk from their mother's mammary glands.

How to Identify Mammals

Mammals are generally secretive in their habits and therefore difficult to spot in the field. The best time to look for mammals is at dusk, dawn and at night, since many retreat to burrows during the day to escape the heat. Some of the best places to look for them are in undisturbed areas affording cover such as wood edges and scrub thickets.

When you spot a mammal, consider its size, shape and color. Check for distinguishing field marks and note the surrounding habitat.

Common Tracks

Studying tracks is an easy way to discover the kinds of mammals found in your area. For more information on animal tracks, see bibliography references under mammals.

Mouse   Opossum   Squirrel   Raccoon

Skunk   Beaver   Bobcat   Porcupine

Elk   Coyote   Mule Deer   Black Bear

N.B. – Tracks are not to scale

MARSUPIALS

Related to kangaroos and koala bears, the opossum is the only marsupial found in North America. Young are born prematurely and move to a fur-lined pouch (marsupium) where they complete their development attached to a teat.

VIRGINIA OPOSSUM
Didelphis virginiana

Size: To 40 in. (1 m)

Description: Distinguished by its long, grayish fur, white face, black-tipped, leathery ears and long, scaly prehensile tail.

Habitat: Woodlands, farming areas, forest edges statewide.

Comments: Most active in the evening and at night, it feeds on a variety of foods, including rodents, rabbits, birds, insects, crustaceans, frogs, fruits, and vegetables. It is the only mammal in the U.S. that has a grasping (prehensile) tail. It has the peculiar habit of pretending to be dead (playing possum) when frightened. Valued for its pelt, it is one of the chief contributors to the Texas fur crop.

ARMADILLOS

The armadillo belongs to a group of mammals that includes sloths and anteaters.

NINE-BANDED ARMADILLO
Dasypus novemcinctus

Size: To 32 in. (80 cm)

Description: Cat-sized mammal is covered with an armored coat consisting of bony plates covered with thin scales.

Habitat: Woodlands, scrubby areas with sandy or soft soil near water.

Comments: A prodigious digger, it will excavate several burrows that serve both as food traps for insects and places to take refuge or rest during the day. When threatened, armadillos may roll into a ball or burrow rapidly. Distinctive tracks are often seen in the mud near water sources. Like the opossum, it often forages near roadways at night. Also called pocket dinosaurs, Hoover hogs and Texas turkeys.

Texas' State Small Mammal

BATS

The only true flying mammals, bats have large ears, small eyes and broad wings. Primarily nocturnal, they have developed a sophisticated sonar system – echolocation – to help them hunt insects at night. As they fly, they emit a series of high frequency sounds that bounce off objects and tell them what lies in their path. During daylight, they seek refuge in caves, trees and attics. Rarely harmful, bats are valuable in helping check insect populations and their excrement (guano) is valuable for the nitrogen it contains.

Long-considered the "battiest" state in the nation, Texas is home to 32 species of bats and many of the largest bat colonies.

Largest Bat Roosts in North America

Bracken Cave near San Antonio, Texas is the summer home to the world's largest colony of bats, with a population estimated at between 20–40 million.

The Congress Avenue Bridge in Austin, Texas is the summer home of 1.5 million Mexican free-tailed bats and is the world's largest urban bat colony.

MEXICAN FREE-TAILED BAT
Tadarida brasiliensis

Size: To 5 in. (13 cm)
Description: Brown bat is distinguished by its tail, which sticks out beyond the tail membrane.
Habitat: Roosts primarily in caves statewide.
Comments: Nests in huge colonies. 'Clouds' of bats can be seen emerging from roosting sites to feed on insects at dusk. The Texas population in summer is estimated at 94–104 million.

Texas' State Flying Mammal

CAVE MYOTIS
Myotis velifer

Size: To 6 in. (15 cm)
Description: Large brown-gray to blackish bat has short ears.
Habitat: Forested areas in western and north-central Texas.
Comments: Colonial, cave-dwelling bat is often found in association with Mexican free-tailed bats. It is the most abundant bat of the Edwards Plateau. Hibernates in central Texas caves in winter.

BIG BROWN BAT
Eptesicus fuscus
Size: To 7 in. (18 cm)
Description: Large bat has thick, glossy yellow-brown fur. Leathery ears are black and rounded.
Habitat: Variable, lives in buildings and trees year-round and hibernates during winter.
Comments: Feeds on insects and is very beneficial controlling agricultural pests like the cucumber beetle.

RED BAT
Lasiurus borealis
Size: To 5 in. (13 cm)
Description: Medium-sized, striking red-orange bat. Females are pinkish brown.
Habitat: Forests throughout Texas.
Comments: Eats insects and roosts singly in deciduous trees in the open. It sometimes hangs by one leg, resembling a dead leaf. It does not use caves, mines or enclosed sites like other species. Migrates to warmer southern areas in winter.

HOARY BAT
Lasiurus cinereus
Size: To 6 in. (15 cm)
Description: Large bat has dense, dark brown fur heavily frosted with white. Note yellow fur around face. Tail membrane is furred.
Habitat: Wooded areas throughout Texas.
Comments: Note large size. Unlike most bats, it is solitary and roosts alone in trees during the day like the red bat. Migrates to South America in winter.

EVENING BAT
Nycticeius humeralis
Size: To 4 in. (10 cm)
Description: Small bat has velvety blackish-brown fur with yellow highlights and small black ears.
Habitat: Forested areas and along waterways in the eastern half of the state.
Comments: Forages in the early evening and at dawn on flying ants, beetles, moths and other insects. Roosts during the day in hollow trees, attics and other man-made structures.

RABBITS & ALLIES

Members of this distinctive group of mammals have long ears, large eyes and long hind legs. They commonly rest in protected areas like thickets during the day. When threatened, they thump their hind feet on the ground as an alarm signal.

BLACK-TAILED JACKRABBIT
Lepus californicus

Size: 20–25 in. (50–63 cm)

Description: Large gray or tan rabbit with long black-tipped ears and a black-streaked tail.

Habitat: Prairies and open areas.

Comments: Very athletic, it hops up to 10 feet (3 m) at a time and can reach speeds of 35 mph (56 kph). Active in late afternoon and evening.

EASTERN COTTONTAIL
Sylvilagus floridanus

Size: To 18 in. (45 cm)

Description: Gray-brown bunny with a white, cottony tail. Nape of neck is rust-colored.

Habitat: Thick brushy areas, fields in the eastern three fourths of the state.

Comments: Feeds primarily on grass. Most active at dawn and dusk, it rests in thickets during the day. Females have up to 7 litters a year of 1–9 young.

DESERT COTTONTAIL
Sylvilagus audubonii

Size: To 16 in. (40 cm)

Description: Buff brown above and white below, it has medium-sized ears and a rusty nape patch. Underside of tail is white.

Habitat: Grasslands and brushy deserts in western Texas.

Comments: In open areas, it will often rest in the burrows of other animals including prairie dogs, badgers and skunks. Often climbs up sloping trees to look for predators.

SWAMP RABBIT
Sylvilagus aquaticus

Size: To 2 ft. (60 cm)

Description: Has coarse brownish fur mottled with black. Feet are rust-colored.

Habitat: Bottomlands, swamps in eastern and coastal Texas.

Comments: An excellent swimmer, it will readily take to water when being pursued. Main predators are dogs, cats and alligators.

SQUIRRELS & ALLIES

This diverse family of hairy-tailed, large-eyed rodents includes chipmunks, tree squirrels, ground squirrels and marmots. Most are active during the day and are easily observed in the field. Note that size includes tail length.

EASTERN GRAY SQUIRREL
Sciurus carolinensis
Size: To 20 in. (50 cm)
Description: Gray squirrel with buff-colored highlights on its face, back and sides.
Habitat: Wooded areas.
Comments: It nests in trees and feeds on a wide variety of nuts, seeds, berries and acorns. Most active in morning and evening.

FOX SQUIRREL
Sciurus niger
Size: To 28 in. (70 cm)
Description: Large squirrel has a long bushy tail. It is gray and black on its back and has an orange belly. Tail is cinnamon and black.
Habitat: Mixed and coniferous forests, swamps.
Comments: Eats mostly nuts, seeds and acorns. The most common squirrel in Texas, it is an important game animal.

SOUTHERN FLYING SQUIRREL
Glaucomys volans
Size: To 10 in. (25 cm)
Description: Large-eyed squirrel is grayish above and light below. Note loose skin membrane connecting its front and rear legs.
Habitat: Forested areas in the eastern third of the state.
Comments: Capable of gliding distances of over 200 ft. (61 m) by spreading its limbs and stretching its flight skin taut. A nocturnal species, it can be heard thumping about in the dark while foraging.

SPOTTED GROUND SQUIRREL
Spermophilus spilosoma
Size: To 9 in. (23 cm)
Description: Coat is pinkish-gray and is covered in small white spots.
Habitat: Dry grasslands and deserts, grassy areas in western and southern Texas.
Comments: Most active in the early morning and late afternoon.

THIRTEEN-LINED GROUND SQUIRREL
Spermophilus tridecemlineatus

Size: To 10 in. (25 cm)

Description: Usually has 13 alternating dark and light stripes down its back.

Habitat: Grasslands, pastures, mountain meadows, roadsides in northern and central Texas.

Comments: Lives in colonies in burrows and feeds primarily on grass and herbs, insects and small vertebrates. Strictly diurnal, studies have shown that it will hibernate during winters for up to 240 days, depending on the temperature.

MEXICAN GROUND SQUIRREL
Spermophilus mexicanus

Size: To 12 in. (30 cm)

Description: Brown rodent usually has nine rows of squarish white spots down its back.

Habitat: Grassy and brushy areas, deserts, roadsides, farmland in southern and western Texas.

Comments: Feeds primarily on leaves, seeds, insects and roadkill carrion. Lives in burrows with multiple entrances.

ROCK SQUIRREL
Otospermophilus variegatus

Size: 17–21 in. (43–53 cm)

Description: Large mottled grayish brown ground squirrel with a long, bushy tail. Coat may be blackish in some parts of the state.

Habitat: Rocky canyons and slopes in central Texas.

Comments: Often seen sitting on rocks, watching for danger. Unlike many ground-dwelling squirrels, it climbs trees easily.

BLACK-TAILED PRAIRIE DOG
Cynomys ludovicianus

Size: To 16 in. (40 cm)

Description: Large, chubby, pinkish-brown burrower has a black-tipped tail.

Habitat: Shortgrass prairies in western Texas.

Comments: Lives in large colonies called prairie dog towns that can have up to several thousand individuals. Active during the day, it is easily observed. Considered a "keystone" species because their colonies create habitats that benefit other species. Noted for their habit of touching noses and incisors when they greet each other that looks like kissing.

POCKET GOPHERS

These mole-like mammals are well known for the mounds of dirt they push up when excavating their burrows. They are named for their fur-lined, external cheek pouches that they stuff with food or nesting material. These pockets can be turned inside out and emptied either into or out of the mouth.

TEXAS POCKET GOPHER
Geomys personatus
Size: To 12.6 in. (32 cm)

Description: A small-eyed, small-eared, "buck-toothed" rodent with a pale-gray back and a belly of mixed gray and white.

Habitat: Underground burrows in mesquite savannas and grasslands with sandy soils.

Comments: Found in the southern part of the state, it is one of nine species of pocket gophers found in Texas. The plains pocket gopher (*G. bursarius*) is found in northern Texas.

Plains Pocket Gopher

SHREWS & MOLES

These small mammals have long snouts, short legs, small eyes and ears and sharp teeth and 5 digits on the front and hind feet. They live on or under the ground and feed on insects and other invertebrates.

DESERT SHREW
Notiosorex crawfordi
Size: 3–4 in. (8–10 cm)

Description: Grayish, mouse-like mammal with a long, pointed nose.

Habitat: Desert scrub in the western two thirds of Texas.

Comments: Obtains water from the insects it feeds on. Like all shrews, it has a very high metabolic rate and may eat up to twice its weight in food each day. One of four species of shrew found in Texas.

EASTERN MOLE
Scalopus aquaticus
Size: To 9 in. (23 cm)

Description: Brownish mammal with a pointed snout and a short naked tail. Front feet have out-turned palms and long claws.

Habitat: Loose soils in the eastern third of Texas.

Comments: Presence can be detected by the mounds of dirt it pushes up when tunneling underground. An expert digger, it can disappear underground in a matter of seconds.

BEAVERS

Found on rivers, lakes and marshes, beavers are the largest North American rodents. Highly aquatic, they have webbed feet and long, broad tails that they slap on the water's surface when alarmed.

AMERICAN BEAVER
Castor canadensis

Size: 40–48 in. (1–1.2 m)
Description: Glossy brown coat, flat, scaly tail.
Habitat: Lakes, ponds and streams.
Comments: Many beavers live in dens excavated along banks; others build cone-shaped houses (lodges) of sticks and mud. Diet consists of the bark of deciduous trees and shrubs, including aspens, willows and maples.

MICE & RATS

Most members of this large group have large ears, long tails and breed throughout the year. Dedicated omnivores, they have adapted to practically every North American habitat. Sizes noted include tail length. There are over 40 species found in Texas.

COMMON MUSKRAT
Ondatra zibethicus

Size: To 2 ft. (60 cm)
Description: Often mistaken for beavers, these glossy brown aquatic rodents are smaller and have a long, scaly tail that is flattened on either side.
Habitat: Marshes, lakes, waterways in northern, southeast and southwest Texas.
Comments: In swampy areas, they construct dome-shaped houses of marsh vegetation up to 3 ft. (90 cm) high. Feeds primarily on aquatic plants. Active year-round.

SOUTHERN PLAINS WOODRAT
Neotoma micropus

Size: To 15 in. (38 cm)
Description: Large rodent is steely gray above and white below with white feet.
Habitat: Dry grasslands with cacti and shrubs in central and western Texas.
Comments: Also called a pack rat, it often builds large houses of sticks, which it uses to cache vegetation and shiny objects it steals from hikers. The eastern woodrat (*N. floridana*) is found in central and eastern Texas.

Eastern Woodrat

BLACK RAT
Rattus rattus
Size: To 18 in. (45 cm)
Description: Black or brownish rodent with a long scaly tail.
Habitat: Dumps, buildings, waste areas.
Comments: Like the house mouse, this species was inadvertently introduced from Europe and is now widespread in North America. It often nests in trees and attics, which earned its other name, the roof rat. Its brownish cousin, the Norway rat (*R. norvegicus*) is also common in Texas near human habitations.

Norway Rat

HOUSE MOUSE
Mus musculus
Size: 5–8 in. (13–20 cm)
Description: Told by its gray coat, large eyes and ears and naked, scaly tail.
Habitat: Very common near human dwellings.
Comments: Normally lives in colonies. Females have up to 5 litters of 4–8 young annually. Estimated population in Texas is in the hundreds of millions.

WHITE-FOOTED MOUSE
Peromyscus leucopus
Size: To 8 in. (20 cm)
Description: Dark brown above, it has orange-brown sides with white undersides and feet. Tail is slightly hairy.
Habitat: Wooded and brushy areas throughout Texas.
Comments: Primarily nocturnal and active year-round. Often seen climbing in trees and shrubs, it feeds on nuts, seeds and fruit as well as caterpillars and insects. The dark brown to gray-brown Texas mouse (*P. attwateri*) is common in central Texas. It is distinguished by its slightly tufted tail.

Texas Mouse

HISPID COTTON RAT
Sigmodon hispidus

Size: To 14 in. (35 cm)

Description: Brown to black rat with coarse, grizzled fur. Tail is less than half the total body length.

Habitat: Meadows, farmlands, ditches.

Comments: Extremely prolific, it begins breeding at six weeks old. One of the most common mammals, it is a major crop pest.

TEXAS KANGAROO RAT
Dipodomys elator

Size: To 16 in. (40 cm)

Description: Large, buff-colored kangaroo rat has long hind legs, silky fur, large eyes and a long, crested tail.

Habitat: Open mesquite scrublands in north-central Texas.

Comments: Currently listed as a vulnerable species, primarily due to loss of habitat. Five similar species are found in Texas. Two of the most widespread are Ord's kangaroo rat (*D. ordii*) and Merriam's kangaroo rat (*D. merriami*) found in western Texas.

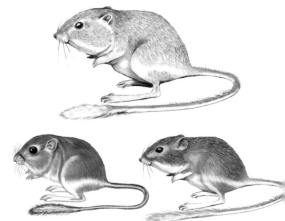

Ord's Kangaroo Rat   Merriam's Kangaroo Rat

PORCUPINES

Porcupines are medium-sized mammals with coats of stiff, barbed quills. When threatened, it faces away from its aggressor, erects its quills and lashes out with its tail. The loosely rooted quills detach on contact and are extremely difficult to remove.

COMMON PORCUPINE
Erethizon dorsatum

Size: 25–37 in. (63–93 cm)

Description: Told by its chunky profile, arched back and long gray coat of barbed quills.

Habitat: Forests, shrubby ravines and sometimes deserts in western Texas.

Comments: Spends much of its time in trees feeding on leaves, twigs and bark. Signs include unique tracks and trees that have large patches of bark removed.

RACCOONS & ALLIES

All members of this diverse family of mammals have ringed tails.

COMMON RACCOON
Procyon lotor

Size: 25–37 in. (63–93 cm)
Description: Easily distinguished by its gray-brown coat, black mask and ringed tail.
Habitat: Wooded areas near water throughout Texas.
Comments: Feeds on small animals, insects, plants and refuse. It often dunks its food into water before eating it. Primarily nocturnal.

RINGTAIL
Bassariscus astutus

Size: 24–32 in. (60–80 cm)
Description: Note large eyes, large ears and a long, ringed tail. Lacks a black mask.
Habitat: Rocky areas, rough country, chaparral.
Comments: Hunts at night, killing prey with a bite to the neck. An expert climber, it is capable of ascending vertical walls. Nicknamed "Miners' Cats," they were once used by miners like house cats to control rodent populations in mines.

WEASELS & ALLIES

Members of this group usually have small heads, long necks, short legs and long bodies. All but sea otters have prominent anal scent glands that are used for social and sexual communication.

LONG-TAILED WEASEL
Mustela frenata

Size: 13–22 in. (33–55 cm)
Description: Told by slender body and long, black-tipped tail. Summer coat is brown above, whitish to yellowish below. Feet are brownish. Those found above 4,000 ft. (1220 m) have a winter coat that is all white except for the black tip on tail.
Habitat: Found near water in open woodlands, meadows and fields.
Comments: Weasels are aggressive hunters and are notorious for killing more prey than they can eat.

NORTHERN RIVER OTTER
Lontra canadensis
Size: To 52 in. (1.3 m)
Description: Torpedo-shaped, glossy brown mammal with short legs, a thick tail and webbed feet.
Habitat: Rivers, ponds and lakes in eastern Texas.
Comments: Active during the day, it spends the majority of its time in or near water. Otters are very playful and often build mud slides on riverbanks. Feeds primarily on fish.

EASTERN SPOTTED SKUNK
Spilogale putorius
Size: To 22 in. (55 cm)
Description: Small black skunk with coat covered with irregular stripes and spots. Tail is white-tipped.
Habitat: Mixed woodlands, wastelands, farmlands.
Comments: When threatened, it gives warning by raising its tail, doing a handstand and spreading its hind feet before spraying. A good climber and swimmer, it is more agile than the striped skunk. The very similar western spotted skunk (*S. gracilis*) is found in the western third of Texas.

Threat display

STRIPED SKUNK
Mephitis mephitis
Size: 20–31 in. (50–78 cm)
Description: Distinguished by its black coat, white forehead stripe and white side stripes. Predominantly white variants also exist.
Habitat: Open wooded areas near water, farmland, suburbs.
Comments: Protects itself by spraying aggressors with noxious smelling fluids from its anal glands. Spray is effective to 15 ft. (5 m) away. Feeds primarily on vegetation, insects and small mammals. The black and white common hog-nosed skunk (*Conepatus leuconotus*) is found in southwestern, central and southern Texas.

Hog-nosed Skunk

MINK
Neovison vison
Size: 20–28 in. (50–70 cm)
Description: Told by rich brown coat; usually has white spotting on chin and throat.
Habitat: Common near water in a variety of habitats in the eastern half of the state.
Comments: Highly aquatic, it dens along river and stream banks and feeds on fish, amphibians, crustaceans and small mammals.

AMERICAN BADGER
Taxidea taxus
Size: 20–34 in. (50–85 cm)
Description: A squat, heavy-bodied animal with a long yellow-gray to brown coat, white forehead stripe and long foreclaws.
Habitat: Grasslands and uncultivated pastures, deserts.
Comments: A prodigious burrower that feeds mostly on rodents but also eats invertebrates, birds, snakes and carrion.

DOG-LIKE MAMMALS

Members of this family have long snouts, erect ears and resemble domestic dogs in looks and habit. All are active year-round.

COYOTE
Canis latrans
Size: To 52 in. (1.3 m)
Description: Yellow-gray with a pointed nose, rust legs and ears and a bushy, black-tipped tail.
Habitat: Wooded and open areas.
Comments: Largely a nocturnal hunter, it is often seen loping across fields at dawn and dusk. Holds tail down when running. Feeds on rodents, rabbits, berries and carrion.

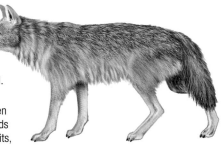

COMMON GRAY FOX
Urocyon cinereoargenteus
Size: 30–44 in. (75–110 cm)
Description: Distinguished by its coat that is blackish-gray above and rusty-white below. Tail has black tip.
Habitat: Deserts, oak woodlands, forests.
Comments: A secretive, nocturnal species, it sometimes forages during the day. An excellent climber, it often seeks refuge in trees.

KIT FOX
Vulpes macrotis

Size: To 34 in. (85 cm)

Description: Slim-bodied fox has large ears and a long, black-tipped tail. Coat is grizzled yellow-gray.

Habitat: Grasslands and deserts in the western third of the state.

Comments: Primarily nocturnal, it can be spotted on roadsides at night in low desert areas. Eats rodents, birds and insects. Once common, it is now in danger of extinction. The similar swift fox (*V. velox*), found in the Trans-Pecos region, has smaller ears and a shorter tail.

Swift Fox

RED FOX
Vulpes vulpes

Size: To 45 in. (1.1 m)

Description: Medium-sized fox has a rusty red coat, black stockings and a long, bushy, white-tipped tail.

Habitat: Woodlands, farms, pastures in northern Texas.

Comments: Active at dawn and dusk, it feeds on rodents, rabbits, wild fruits and berries, and insects. Introduced to Texas for sport in 1895, it is well-distributed but not common anywhere.

CAT-LIKE MAMMALS

These highly specialized carnivores are renowned hunters. All have short faces, keen vision, powerful bodies and retractable claws. Most are nocturnal hunters.

BOBCAT
Lynx rufus

Size: 3–4 ft. (.9–1.2 m)

Description: Key field marks are its spotted red-brown coat, short tail and tufted ears.

Habitat: Scrubby open woodlands, thickets, and swamps statewide.

Comments: Named for its bobbed tail, it rests in thickets by day and hunts rabbits, rodents and birds by night.

MOUNTAIN LION
Puma concolor

Size: 5–9 ft. (1.5–2.7 m)
Description: Large tan cat has a whitish belly and long, black-tipped tail.
Habitat: Primarily mountainous areas in the Trans-Pecos region.
Comments: A solitary hunter, it feeds on hoofed mammals, hares and other small mammals. Also called cougar and puma.

HOOFED MAMMALS

This general grouping includes odd- and even-toed hoofed mammals from a variety of families.

WHITE-TAILED DEER
Odocoileus virginianus

Size: 6–7 ft. (1.8–2.1 m)
Description: Coat is tan in summer, grayish in winter. Named for its large, white-edged tail which is held aloft, flag-like, when running.
Habitat: Forests, farmlands and river valleys.
Comments: An agile, elusive deer, it can reach speeds of 40 mph (65 kph) and leap obstacles as high as 8 ft. (2.5 m). Most active at dawn and dusk. The most important Texas game animal, the population is estimated at 3 million. The mule deer (*O. hemionus*) is found principally in the Trans-Pecos and Panhandle region. It has a narrow, black-tipped tail and very large ears.

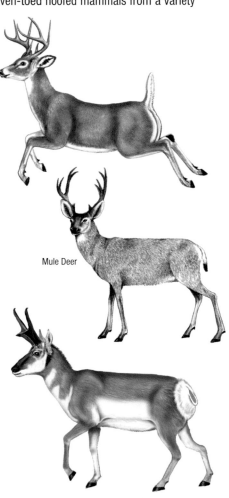

Mule Deer

PRONGHORN
Antilocapra americana

Size: 4–5 ft. (1.2–1.5 m)
Description: A tan, deer-like animal with white throat bands, a white rump and stumpy, pronged horns.
Habitat: Grasslands and sagebrush flats in the Panhandle and Trans-Pecos regions.
Comments: The fastest animal in North America, it has been clocked at speeds up to 70 mph (112 kph).

MOUNTAIN SHEEP
Ovis canadensis
Size: 5–6 ft. (1.5–1.8 m)
Description: Told by large coiled horns and white rump patch.
Habitat: Semi-open steep terrain in rocky areas in mountains and deserts.
Comments: A powerful climber, it has specialized 'suction-cup' hooves that enhance its traction on rocky slopes. Extirpated in Texas in 1959, it is being reintroduced to sanctuaries in west Texas.

JAVELINA
Pecari tajacu
Size: 34–40 in. (85–100 cm)
Description: Pig-like animal with a dark, bristly coat and a pale collar stripe.
Habitat: Well-vegetated deserts in western and southern Texas.
Comments: Feeds on cacti, seeds, fruit, small animals (including snakes, birds and rodents) and invertebrates. Primarily nocturnal.

MARINE MAMMALS

This group includes mammals that live in or on the water. The fish-like dolphins and whales spend all of their time in the water. Finned marine mammals are easily distinguished from fishes because their tails have horizontal, rather than vertical, flukes.

BOTTLENOSED DOLPHIN
Tursiops truncatus
Size: To 12 ft. (3.6 m)
Description: Distinguished by its large size, gray color and short beak.
Habitat: Coastal and offshore waters.
Comments: The most common dolphin in Gulf waters, it is often found in shallow coastal waters and estuaries.

ATLANTIC SPOTTED DOLPHIN
Stenella frontalis
Size: To 7.5 ft. (2.3 m)
Description: Smallish purplish-gray dolphin is covered in gray to white spots on its sides and back.
Habitat: Coastal and offshore waters.
Comments: Also called Gulf Stream dolphin.

BEARS

Heavy-bodied, large-headed mammals have short ears and small tails.

BLACK BEAR
Ursus americanus

Size: 4–6 ft. (1.2–1.8 m)

Description: Coat is normally black, but cinnamon, dark brown and blond variants also occur. Snout is straight and muzzle is brown.

Habitat: Primarily forested areas.

Comments: Diet is 95% vegetarian and consists of berries, acorns, grasses and forbs. Black bear populations are recovering in Texas and currently there are bears in the Big Bend area of the Trans-Pecos, the western Hill Country, the Panhandle, and deep northeast Texas.

INTRODUCED SPECIES

NUTRIA
Myocastor coypus

Size: To 4 ft. (1.2 m)

Description: Large brown semi-aquatic rodent with a long round tail.

Habitat: Marshes, streams, ponds in the eastern two thirds of the state.

Comments: Introduced from South America for fur-farming, nutrias are now widespread and outcompete many native species for food and habitats. An invasive species, it causes considerable crop damage. It often feeds on land and when disturbed enters the water with a loud splash.

WILD HOG
Sus scrofa

Size: To 6 ft. (1.8 m)

Description: Usually black, pig-like animal has a long grizzled coat and tusks up to 9 in. (23 cm) long. Tail hangs straight and is not coiled.

Habitat: Swamps, brushlands.

Comments: Introduced by ranchers and sportsmen in the 1930s, it is a descendant of escaped domestic hogs or European wild hogs. One of the worst invasive species in Texas, it devastates large tracts of land by uprooting vegetation and causing excessive erosion. It also devours many native animals including endangered species.

AXIS DEER
Axis axis

Size: To 5.5 ft. (1.7 m)

Description: Distinguished by its white-spotted, reddish coat and white throat. Male antlers sweep backward with an upward curve and usually have three tines off the main beam and are up to 40 in. (1 m) long.

Habitat: Grasslands, open woodlands.

Comments: Native to India and Ceylon, it was introduced to Texas in 1932 and is now the most common exotic in Texas. There are now over 6,000 free-ranging animals and 40,000 kept on ranches in 92 counties. Also known as chital, cheetal and spotted deer.

FALLOW DEER
Dama dama

Size: To 6 ft. (1.8 m)

Description: Medium-sized deer has large palmate antlers up to 16 in. (40 cm) long. Coat color varies from black to red, brown or white.

Habitat: Grasslands and open woodlands.

Comments: Native to the Mediterranean countries of Europe and north Africa, it is found free-ranging in one county and confined on ranches in 93 counties. Population is estimated at over 15,000.

BLACKBUCK
Antilope cervicapra

Size: To 4 ft. (1.2 m)

Description: Medium-sized brown-black and white deer. Male has unbranched "corkscrew" V-shaped horns that are up to 32 in. (80 cm) long. Note white eye ring and white on chin, chest, belly and inner legs. Females and juveniles are tan-colored.

Habitat: Mostly found in the Texas Hill Country, it browses on bushes and low trees.

Comments: Native to Pakistan and India, it was originally released in the Edwards Plateau in 1932. Confined populations are found in 86 counties and the current population is estimated over 25,000.

SIKA DEER
Cervus nippon

Size: To 5 ft. (1.5 m)

Description: Compact, dainty-legged deer has a wedge-shaped head. Male antlers have a main beam with 3–4 tines and are up to 30 in. (75 cm) long. Due to excessive hybridization, size and coloration are highly variable.

Habitat: Broadleaf and mixed forests.

Comments: Native to Japan and southern Siberia, it is confined on ranches in 77 counties in central and southern Texas. The current population is estimated to be over 14,000.

NILGAI (BLUE BULL)
Boselaphus tragocamelus

Size: To 6.5 ft. (2 m)

Description: Large, robust ungulate has smooth, short horns and white facial and "bib" patches. Prominent withers makes the back slope from the shoulder to the rump. Males are gray to brown-gray while females are brown to orange-brown.

Habitat: Dry grasslands, scrubby areas, open woodlands.

Comments: Native to Pakistan and India, it was introduced to Texas in 1930. Nearly 40,000 animals are found in Texas with many free-ranging animals found in south Texas. Usually found in small herds of 10–20. Males can weigh up to 679 lbs. (308 kg).

BARBARY SHEEP (AOUDAD)
Ammotragus lervia

Size: To 6 ft. (1.8 m)

Description: Large sheep has prominent horns that curve outward, backward and then inward. Has conspicuous growth of long hair on throat, chest and upper front legs.

Habitat: Dry, rough, barren areas.

Comments: An expert climber, it can easily ascend and descend steep, rocky slopes. Native to north Africa, it was introduced to Texas in 1957. It is free-ranging in a few areas and confined on ranches in 65 counties. Current population is estimated at over 20,000.

TEXAS LONGHORN
Bos taurus

Size: To 5 ft. (1.5 m)

Description: Easily distinguished by its massive horns, which can be over 10 ft. (3 m) long. Coat is variable in color and usually spotted.

Habitat: Grasslands, open woodlands.

Comments: This hardy bovine, which can thrive on weeds and brush in areas where no other cattle could survive, is the only breed of cattle to evolve without human influence. Originally a hybrid of two ancient cattle lineages from India and the Middle East, it is a direct descendant of the first cattle brought to the New World by Christopher Columbus.

Texas' State Large Mammal

Birds are warm-blooded, feathered animals with two wings and two legs. The majority can fly and those that cannot are believed to be descended from ancestors that did. Adaptations for flight include hollow bones and an enhanced breathing capacity. Birds also have an efficient four-chambered heart and are insulated against the weather to enhance temperature regulation.

How to Identify Birds

As with other species, the best way to become good at identifying birds is simply to practice. The more birds you attempt to identify, the better you will become at distinguishing species.

When birding, the first thing to note is the habitat you are exploring in order to know what kinds of birds to expect. When you spot a bird, check for obvious field marks. Note the shape of its silhouette and beak. Note the color and pattern of its feathers for distinguishing markings at rest and in flight. Is it small (sparrow), medium (crow), or large (heron)? Does it have any unusual behavioral characteristics?

If you are interested in enhancing your field skills, it is essential to become familiar with bird songs since many species that are difficult to observe in the field are readily identified by their distinctive song. Bird song apps and CDs are available online and from nature stores and libraries.

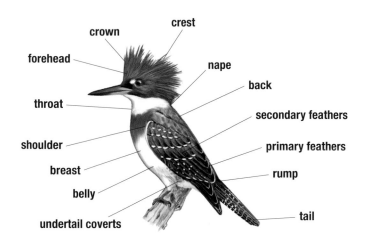

N.B. – It is important to note that most species illustrations in this guide feature the adult male in its breeding coloration. Colors and markings shown may be duller or absent during different times of the year.

DUCKS & ALLIES

Smaller than geese, ducks have shorter necks and are primarily aquatic. In most, breeding males are more brightly colored than females. Both sexes have a brightly colored band (speculum) on the trailing edge of the wing.

WOOD DUCK
Aix sponsa

Size: To 20 in. (50 cm)

Description: Multi-colored, crested male has a green head, white neck, red eyes and red bill. Female is dull-colored with a white eye patch.

Habitat: Wooded ponds, marshes, lakes, rivers.

Comments: Often seen perching in trees, it is one of a few ducks to nest in tree cavities.

NORTHERN PINTAIL
Anas acuta

Size: 20–30 in. (50–75 cm)

Description: Distinguished by its long neck and pointed tail. Male has a brown head and a white breast and neck stripe. Both sexes have a glossy brown speculum that is bordered in white.

Habitat: Shallow marshes and ponds.

Comments: Call is a short whistle.

AMERICAN WIGEON
Mareca americana

Size: 18–23 in. (45–58 cm)

Description: Male is brownish with a gray head and a glossy green face patch. Female has a bluish bill and flecked head. Speculum is green.

Habitat: Freshwater streams, lakes, marshes.

Comments: Although primarily aquatic, this duck can often be found nibbling grass on the shores of ponds and marshes.

NORTHERN SHOVELER
Spatula clypeata
Size: 17–20 in. (43–50 cm)

Description: Told by its flat head and large, spatulate bill. Male has a green head, rusty sides and a blue wing patch.

Habitat: Fresh- and saltwater marshes, lakes, ponds.

Comments: Shovel-shaped bill is used to strain aquatic animals and vegetation from the water. Swims with bill pointed downward.

GREEN-WINGED TEAL
Anas crecca
Size: 12–16 in. (30–40 cm)

Description: Male has chestnut-colored head and a green eye patch. Female is brown-gray. Speculum is green.

Habitat: Inland lakes, ponds and streams.

Comments: The smallest North American dabbling duck. Flies in tight flocks that move in unison.

BLUE-WINGED TEAL
Anas discors
Size: 15–16 in. (38–40 cm)

Description: Male has a gray-blue head with a white facial crescent. Female is mottled brown.

Habitat: Ponds, marshes, estuaries.

Comments: A dabbling duck, it feeds by tipping over (tail in the air) when foraging for plants, aquatic insects and mollusks.

MALLARD
Anas platyrhynchos
Size: 20–28 in. (50–70 cm)

Description: Male has a green head, white collar and chestnut breast. Female is mottled brown. Both have a metallic blue speculum.

Habitat: Ponds, marshes, bays.

Comments: The ancestor of domestic ducks. Male's call is a loud – *quack*.

BLACK-BELLIED WHISTLING DUCK
Dendrocygna autumnalis
Size: To 22 in. (55 cm)

Description: Goose-like duck has long red-pink legs, a long neck, gray head and white eye ring. Sexes are similar.

Habitat: Tree-lined streams and ponds.

Comments: Named for its whistling call. Common summer resident on the south Texas coastal plain.

RUDDY DUCK
Oxyura jamaicensis
Size: To 16 in. (40 cm)

Description: Small duck has a chestnut body, white cheek and blue bill. Mottled brownish female has a dark line beneath the eye. The male's tail is often cocked in the air when swimming.

Habitat: Lakes, ponds, rivers.

Comments: Diving duck has stiff tail feathers that serve as a rudder.

♀

♂

MOTTLED DUCK
Anas fulvigula
Size: To 20 in. (50 cm)

Description: Mottled brown duck is similar to the female mallard but has a yellower bill and darker tail. Blue-green speculum lacks a white border along the leading edge. Sexes are similar.

Habitat: Marshes, prairies.

Comments: One of the most frequently banded ducks along the Gulf of Mexico.

♀

♂

GREBES

The members of this group of duck-like birds have short tails, slender necks and stiff bills. Excellent divers, they have lobed toes rather than webbed feet.

PIED-BILLED GREBE
Podilymbus podiceps
Size: To 13 in. (33 cm)

Description: Small brown bird with a stout, ringed bill and a dark throat.

Habitat: Marshes, ponds.

Comments: Often swims partially submerged. Also called dabchick, devil-diver, and hell-diver. Unique vocalization sounds like a whooping – *kuk-kuk-cow-cow-cow-cowp-cowp*.

COOTS & ALLIES

Coots are chicken-billed birds often found in the company of ducks and geese. They are, however, more closely related to cranes than ducks.

AMERICAN COOT
Fulica americana
Size: 13–16 in. (33–40 cm)
Description: Black bird is easily distinguished by its white, banded bill. Legs are long and greenish. Sexes are similar.
Habitat: Fresh water in the summer and fresh- and saltwater in winter.
Comments: Feeds on the shore and in the water. Habitually pumps its head back and forth when swimming. Large flocks congregate in shallow marshes during winter.

COMMON GALLINULE
Gallinula galeata
Size: To 14 in. (35 cm)
Description: Dark bird has an orange forehead shield, a red, yellow-tipped bill and yellow feet with extremely long toes.
Habitat: Well-vegetated freshwater marshes and ponds.
Comments: Long toes allow it to walk on lily pads without sinking. Constantly bobs its head while swimming. Also called moorhen. The colorful purple gallinule (*Porphyrio martinicus*) is found in southern and eastern Texas in spring and summer.

Purple Gallinule

GEESE

Geese are large, long-necked birds found near ponds and marshes. Highly terrestrial, they are often spotted grazing in fields and meadows. Their diet consists largely of grasses, grains and some aquatic plants. Noisy in flight, they are often heard before they are seen passing overhead.

CANADA GOOSE
Branta canadensis
Size: 24–45 in. (60–114 cm)
Description: Large bird has a black head and neck and white chin strap.
Habitat: Near marshes, ponds, lakes, rivers and estuaries.
Comments: Flocks usually fly in Vs when migrating. Feeds primarily on grasses, seeds and insects in wetlands, grasslands and agricultural areas. Pairs usually mate for life. Call is a nasal – *honk*.

LARGE WADING & NEARSHORE BIRDS

This general category includes birds from a variety of families. Most inhabit marshes, estuaries and/or coastal waters where they feed on fishes, frogs and insects.

GREAT EGRET
Ardea alba
Size: 35–40 in. (.9–1 m)
Description: Large white bird with a yellow bill, black legs and black feet. Has shaggy white plumes on breast during breeding season.
Habitat: Fresh and salt marshes, tidal flats, flooded fields.
Comments: Feeds mainly on fish, frogs and small mammals that it spears with its long, sharp bill. Call is a deep croak.

SNOWY EGRET
Egretta thula
Size: 20–27 in. (50–70 cm)
Description: Small white heron is easily distinguished by its black bill and yellow feet. Note yellow patch of skin at base of bill.
Habitat: Marshes, ponds, swamps, estuaries and mudflats.
Comments: When feeding, it will often run after its prey with wings spread.

CATTLE EGRET
Bubulcus ibis
Size: To 20 in. (50 cm)
Description: Small, stocky heron has buff feathers on its crown, breast and back during breeding season.
Habitat: Open fields and pastures near ponds and swamps.
Comments: Often found near livestock, it feeds on the insects they stir up while grazing.

GREEN HERON
Butorides virescens
Size: To 22 in. (55 cm)
Description: Gray-green wading bird has a chestnut neck, a black crown and yellow legs.
Habitat: Ponds, streams, brackish marshes.
Comments: Often spotted perching on branches near water. Is known to drop "bait" into the water to attract fish.

LITTLE BLUE HERON
Egretta caerulea

Size: 25–30 in. (65–75 cm)

Description: Small heron has a slate blue body, a maroon neck and a blue or grayish bill with a black tip.

Habitat: Swamps, lagoons and coastal thickets.

Comments: Is a permanent resident along the coastal plain of Texas.

TRICOLORED HERON
Egretta tricolor

Size: 25–30 in. (65–75 cm)

Description: Long-billed, small, gray-blue heron has a white belly and foreneck and tawny plumes on its back.

Habitat: Salt marshes, coastal swamps.

Comments: Also known as the Louisiana heron, it is a common permanent resident along the coast.

GREAT BLUE HERON
Ardea herodias

Size: To 4.5 ft. (1.4 m)

Description: Very large gray-blue bird with long yellow legs, a yellowish, dagger-like bill and whitish face. Note the black plumes extending back from the eye.

Habitat: The borders of rivers, streams and lakes.

Comments: Creates huge nests in tall trees. Despite its massive wings that can span up to 6 ft., adults weigh a mere 5–7 lbs. (2.2–3.1 kg).

BLACK-CROWNED NIGHT-HERON
Nycticorax nycticorax

Size: 23–28 in. (58–70 cm)

Description: Stocky bird has a black crown and back, red eyes and short yellow legs. The long plumes extend from the back of the head and are shown during greeting and courtship displays.

Habitat: Marshes, swamps, wooded waterways.

Comments: Stands quietly along shorelines for long periods waiting for fish or frogs to pass by. Also raids the nests of other birds at night.

YELLOW-CROWNED NIGHT-HERON
Nyctanassa violacea

Size: 22–27 in. (55–70 cm)

Description: Gray heron has a black head, white cheeks and yellowish crown and plumes.

Habitat: Coastal thickets, wooded swamps.

Comments: Unlike other herons, it feeds primarily on crabs and crayfish, which it can crush with its stout bill.

ROSEATE SPOONBILL
Platalea ajaja

Size: To 32 in. (80 cm)

Description: White-pinkish wading bird has unique bill with a flattened, spoon-shaped tip.

Habitat: Mangrove keys, estuaries, mudflats, lagoons.

Comments: It swings its bill from side to side in shallow water while feeding on small fish, crustaceans and insects. Flies with its legs and neck outstretched.

AMERICAN WHITE PELICAN
Pelecanus erythrorhynchos

Size: 55–70 in. (1.4–1.8 m)

Description: Large, stout white bird has a long bill and an orange-yellow throat pouch. Wing tips are black. Breeding adult has a yellowish crest on its bill.

Habitat: Lakes and coastal lagoons.

Comments: Often travels in flocks that fly in a V-formation. Feeds by scooping small schooling fish into its throat pouch.

BROWN PELICAN
Pelecanus occidentalis

Size: To 50 in. (1.3 m)

Description: Very large stocky bird has a brownish body, a long, pouched beak, white head (often washed with yellow) and chestnut hindneck.

Habitat: Coastal beaches and lagoons.

Comments: Common resident feeds by plunging from great heights into the water for fish.

ANHINGA
Anhinga anhinga
Size: To 3 ft. (90 cm)
Description: Large black bird with long, snaking neck, pointed bill and a long tail. Females have a tan neck. Note silvery wing patches.
Habitat: Marshes, swamps, lakes.
Comments: Often perches with wings outspread to let them dry. Slender bill is used to skewer fish while swimming underwater. Also called snakebird, it frequently swims with only its head and bill above water.

SANDHILL CRANE
Grus canadensis
Size: To 4 ft. (1.2 m)
Description: Long-legged gray wading bird has a red forecrown and white cheeks.
Habitat: Freshwater marshes, pastures.
Comments: Unlike herons, cranes fly with their necks outstretched. Often occurs in large flocks during breeding season. Over half a million migrate through Nebraska each spring. The endangered whooping crane (*G. americana*) winters along the gulf coast of Texas.

Whooping Crane

WOOD STORK
Mycteria americana
Size: To 4 ft. (1.2 m)
Description: Large white bird has a naked, gray, scaly head and neck and a downcurved bill.
Habitat: Swamps, ponds and coastal shallows.
Comments: Feeds primarily on fish, crabs, insects and frogs. Formerly called the wood ibis, it was once endangered and populations are slowly recovering.

WHITE IBIS
Eudocimus albus
Size: To 28 in. (70 cm)
Description: Key field marks are white plumage, reddish legs and reddish, downturned bill. Black wing tips are evident in flight.
Habitat: Swamps, marshes, prairies, estuaries.
Comments: Nests, roosts and feeds in large colonies near lakes and swamps. The white-faced ibis (*Plegadis chihi*) breeds and winters along the gulf coast.

White-faced Ibis

DOUBLE-CRESTED CORMORANT
Phalacrocorax auritus
Size: To 3 ft. (90 cm)
Description: Glossy black bird with a slender neck, hooked bill and orange throat pouch.
Habitat: Lakes, rivers, swamps and coastal waters.
Comments: Nests in colonies and is often seen perched on trees and pilings near marinas. Often perches with wings outstretched to allow them to dry.

NEOTROPIC CORMORANT
Phalacrocorax brasilianus
Size: To 25 in. (63 cm)
Description: Small black-olive glossy cormorant has an orange throat patch bordered in white.
Habitat: Brackish and freshwater wetlands.
Comments: Grunt call is pig-like. Also known as olivaceous cormorant or Mexican cormorant, it is primarily a coastal species in Texas.

SHOREBIRDS & ALLIES

This general category includes wading birds normally found along shorelines. Many have slender bills which they use to probe the sand and mud for invertebrates.

SANDERLING
Calidris alba
Size: To 8 in. (20 cm)
Description: Brown above, white below with black legs and a black bill. In winter, they are grayish.
Habitat: Seashores, mudflats.
Comments: Common resident along the coast, it runs in and out with the surf, probing its bill in the wet sand in search of invertebrates.

KILLDEER
Charadrius vociferus
Size: To 12 in. (30 cm)
Description: Thick-necked, short-billed bird with a brown back, white breast and two black breast bands. Rump shows orange in flight.
Habitat: Seashore, fields, pastures, parks, open areas.
Comments: Feigns a broken wing when young in nest are approached. Shrill call – *kill-dee, kill-dee* – is repeated continuously.

AMERICAN OYSTERCATCHER
Haematopus palliatus
Size: 17–21 in. (43–53 cm)
Description: Distinguished by its brown back, white underparts, black head and stout orange bill.
Habitat: Beaches, mudflats.
Comments: Feeds primarily on shellfish. Call is a shrill – *kleeep*.

BLACK-NECKED STILT
Himantopus mexicanus
Size: To 17 in. (43 cm)
Description: Easily distinguished by its black and white plumage and long, thin legs, neck and bill.
Habitat: Shorelines of fresh- and saltwater.
Comments: Call is a repetitive series of piping notes.

LONG-BILLED CURLEW
Numenius americanus
Size: To 23 in. (58 cm)
Description: Large, heavy-bodied shorebird has a long, decurved bill.
Habitat: Prairies, pastures, lawns.
Comments: Call is a musical, ascending – *cur-lee.* Found in all but the eastern quarter of Texas, it is a common winter resident on the coastal plain.

AMERICAN AVOCET
Recurvirostra americana
Size: To 20 in. (50 cm)
Description: Large shorebird with long legs and a long upcurved bill. Breeding birds have a tawny head and neck.
Habitat: Shallow ponds, marshes, estuaries, flooded pastures.
Comments: Feeds by swinging bill side to side while walking through the water. Call is – *kleet-kleet-kleet.*

GREATER YELLOWLEGS
Tringa melanoleuca
Size: To 15 in. (38 cm)

LESSER YELLOWLEGS
Tringa flavipes
Size: To 10 in. (25 cm)

Description: Distinguished from other shorebirds by its large size and long, bright yellow legs. The greater yellowlegs is taller and has a thicker bill that may be upturned slightly.

Habitat: Coastal wetlands, lake and pond margins.

Comments: The calls of the two species are distinctive; the greater has a rapid, descending three note call – *tew, tew, tew* – while the lesser's is one- or two-notes – *pew-pew* – of the same pitch.

SPOTTED SANDPIPER
Actitis macularius
Size: To 8 in. (20 cm)
Description: Gray-brown above and white below, it has dark-spotted underparts.
Habitat: Streams, ponds, rivers, lakes and beaches statewide.
Comments: Constantly teeters when foraging. Call is – *peet-weet*.

WILLET
Tringa semipalmata
Size: To 17 in. (43 cm)
Description: Large shorebird is mottled gray-brown above. Wings flash black and white in flight.
Habitat: Estuaries, beaches, marshes, mudflats.
Comments: Common resident along the coast. Has several raucous calls including the name-saying – *pill-will-willet*.

RUDDY TURNSTONE
Arenaria interpres
Size: To 10 in. (25 cm)
Description: Plump shorebird is rufous above, white below with a black breast and black and white facial pattern.
Habitat: Mudflats, beaches.
Comments: Distinctive call is a low guttural rattle or a single, whistled – *tew*. Common migrant in spring and autumn.

GULLS & ALLIES

These long-winged birds are strong fliers and excellent swimmers. Gulls are usually gray and white and have webbed feet and square tails; immature birds are brownish. Terns are smaller with narrow wings, forked tails and pointed bills.

Herring Gull

RING-BILLED GULL
Larus delawarensis
Size: To 20 in. (50 cm)
Description: Key field marks are a black-ringed bill, yellow eyes, yellow legs and a dark-tipped white tail.
Habitat: Found near lakes, rivers, fields, dumps and shopping malls.
Comments: Varied diet includes carrion, garbage, eggs, young birds and aquatic animals. The herring gull (*L. argentatus smithsonianus*) has pink legs and a red bill spot. It is a common coastal resident in winter.

LAUGHING GULL
Leucophaeus atricilla
Size: To 18 in. (45 cm)
Description: Small coastal gull has a dark gray mantle and black wing tips. Head is black in summer, white with a dark smudge in winter.
Habitat: Marshes, bays, beaches, piers.
Comments: A year-round resident of Texas. Call resembles a loud laugh – *ha-ha-ha*.

FORSTER'S TERN
Sterna forsteri
Size: To 15 in. (38 cm)
Description: Gray above and white below, it has an orange or yellow bill with a black tip and a forked tail.
Habitat: Marshes, bays, beaches.
Comments: Common permanent resident along the coast.

BLACK SKIMMER
Rynchops niger
Size: To 20 in. (50 cm)
Description: Distinguished by black and white plumage, long wings and long, black-tipped, orange bill. The lower bill is longer than the upper.
Habitat: Common summer resident along the coast.
Comments: Feeds by flying with its lower bill cutting water; when it feels a fish, the upper bill snaps down. Often flies in flocks. Call resembles a dog's bark.

HAWKS, EAGLES & ALLIES

Primarily carnivorous, these birds have sharp talons for grasping prey and sharply hooked bills for tearing into flesh. Many soar on wind currents when hunting. Sexes are similar in most.

RED-TAILED HAWK
Buteo jamaicensis
Size: 20–25 in. (50–63 cm)
Description: Dark, broad-winged, wide-tailed hawk with light underparts and a red tail. Dark belly band is visible in flight.
Habitat: Open fields and forests, farmlands.
Comments: This familiar hawk is often spotted perched on roadside poles and fence posts.

CRESTED CARACARA
Caracara cheriway
Size: To 25 in. (63 cm)
Description: Key field marks are black head crest, red face and long legs.
Habitat: Open woodlands, prairies.
Comments: Often seen running along the ground in search of prey. It also eats carrion and is dominant over vultures at kill sites.

TURKEY VULTURE
Cathartes aura
Size: To 32 in. (80 cm)
Description: Large soaring bird with brown-black plumage and a naked red head. Trailing edge of wing feathers are lighter colored giving the bird a two-toned look from below.
Habitat: Dry, open country.
Comments: Feeds on carrion and is often seen along roadsides. Often seen soaring when foraging, it has a V-shaped flight profile.

BLACK VULTURE
Coragyps atratus
Size: 22–26 in. (55–65 cm)
Description: Large black bird has a naked black head and a short tail. Silvery wing tips are evident in flight.
Habitat: Open country, woodlands.
Comments: Does not soar like the turkey vulture but flaps and glides at lower elevations. Common resident in the eastern half of Texas.

OSPREY
Pandion haliaetus
Size: 20–25 in. (50–63 cm)
Description: Large raptor has a dark brown back, light underparts and a dark eye stripe.
Habitat: Coastal, inland lakes and rivers.
Comments: Unlike most soaring birds, it glides with its wings arched. Often hovers over the water before diving after fish. Its unusual talons allow it to grasp prey with two toes in front and two behind.

HARRIS'S HAWK
Parabuteo unicinctus
Size: 18–23 in. (45–58 cm)
Description: Dark brown hawk has chestnut shoulders and thighs. Has white at base of tail and on tail tip.
Habitat: Semi-arid, scrubby areas, it is a common resident in south, central and west Texas.
Comments: A sit-and-wait predator, it is often seen perched on telephone and utility poles along highways.

AMERICAN KESTREL
Falco sparverius
Size: To 12 in. (30 cm)
Description: Small falcon has a rust back and tail and pointed, narrow, spotted blue wings. Males have dark facial marks.
Habitat: Wooded and open areas.
Comments: Formerly called the sparrow hawk, it is often seen perched on utility lines or fences along roadways.

RED-SHOULDERED HAWK
Buteo lineatus
Size: To 22 in. (55 cm)
Description: Brown hawk has rust shoulder patches, brown and white barred wings and a white-banded tail.
Habitat: Deciduous woods, pine scrub, swamps in the eastern half of Texas.
Comments: Hunts from a perch for prey including snakes, frogs, rodents and birds. Call is a shrill scream – *kee-yeear* – with a downward inflection.

NORTHERN HARRIER
Circus hudsonius
Size: 18–24 in. (45–61 cm)

Description: Slim, long-tailed and long-winged hawk is gray above and pale and spotted below. White rump is conspicuous in flight. Note V-shaped flight profile.

Habitat: Marshes, grasslands.

Comments: Flies a few feet above the ground, often hovering, as it hunts rodents and other small prey.

SHARP-SHINNED HAWK
Accipiter striatus
Size: 10–14 in. (25–35 cm)

Description: Plumage is gray above and light below. Underparts are barred with brownish-orange stripes. Females tend to be browner than males.

Habitat: Forests.

Comments: The smallest hawk, it has short, rounded wings that enable it to maneuver through dense woods when hunting.

COOPER'S HAWK
Accipiter cooperii
Size: 14–20 in. (35–50 cm)

Description: Distinguished from the similar, smaller sharp-shinned hawk by its size and rounded, notched tail.

Habitat: Mixed woodlands.

Comments: These birds are common in urban areas and feed primarily on songbirds and small animals.

BALD EAGLE
Haliaeetus leucocephalus
Size: To 40 in. (1 m)

Description: Large dark bird with white head and tail, and yellow legs and bill. Juveniles are brown and take 4–5 years to attain adult plumage.

Habitat: Near rivers, lakes, estuaries.

Comments: Feeds primarily on fish but also eats a wide variety of animals and carrion. A threatened species in Texas. Breeding birds are found in the eastern half of the state whereas wintering birds are located primarily in the Panhandle, central and east Texas.

Juvenile

CHICKEN-LIKE BIRDS

Ground-dwelling birds that are chicken-like in looks and habit. Most have stout bills, rounded wings and heavy bodies. Primarily ground-dwelling, they are capable of short bursts of flight.

WILD TURKEY
Meleagris gallopavo
Size: To 4 ft. (1.2 m)
Description: Resembles a slim domestic turkey. Males have blue to pink facial patches and red fleshy wattles under the bill.
Habitat: Open woodlands, hammocks, prairies.
Comments: Males are often heard 'gobbling' at dawn as they gather the females in their flock. Most roost in trees at night.

RING-NECKED PHEASANT
Phasianus colchicus
Size: To 3 ft. (90 cm)
Description: Stunning red-faced, green headed bird has an extremely long tail.
Habitat: Pastures, agricultural fields.
Comments: Permanent resident of the Panhandle, it has been introduced throughout the state. The pheasant-like plain chachalaca (*Ortalis vetula*) is found in the Lower Rio Grande Valley.

Plain Chachalaca

NORTHERN BOBWHITE
Colinus virginianus
Size: To 12 in. (30 cm)
Description: A small, plump brown bird with a small head and short tail. Males have a white throat and eye stripe.
Habitat: Open woodlands, roadsides, wood edges, brushy fields.
Comments: This ground dweller is often flushed by hikers. Call is a clear – *bob-WHITE*!

SWIFTS & ALLIES

Aerial feeders, they are speedy, acrobatic fliers with wide-opening mouths.

CHIMNEY SWIFT
Chaetura pelagica
Size: To 6 in. (15 cm)
Description: Gray-brown bird has long, sickle-shaped wings.
Habitat: Forests, towns, open country.
Comments: Nests and roosts in chimneys. Has rapid, bat-like flight where wings appear to beat alternately.

HUMMINGBIRDS

The smallest birds, hummingbirds are named for the noise made by their wings during flight. All have long, needle-like bills and long tongues which are used to extract nectar from flowers.

BLACK-CHINNED HUMMINGBIRD
Archilochus alexandri

Size: 3–4 in. (8–10 cm)
Description: Small metallic green bird with a black chin and a purplish neck band. Females lack chin and neck markings.
Habitat: Urban areas, wooded canyons to middle elevations.
Comments: Widespread throughout most of Texas, many winter on the Gulf Coast.

RUBY-THROATED HUMMINGBIRD
Archilochus colubris

Size: To 3.5 in. (9 cm)
Description: Plumage is green above, whitish below. Only male has a bright red throat.
Habitat: Forests, cities.
Comments: Often found hovering in meadows and gardens near flowers. When defending its territory, male will often swoop down to "buzz" intruders.

KINGFISHERS

Solitary, broad-billed birds renowned for their fishing expertise.

BELTED KINGFISHER
Megaceryle alcyon

Green Kingfisher

Size: To 14 in. (35 cm)
Description: Stocky blue-gray bird with a large crested head and a long, stout bill.
Habitat: Near clear water.
Comments: Often seen perched on powerlines or in trees near water. Usually hovers over water before plunging after fish. The smaller green kingfisher (*Chloroceryle americana*) is found in central Texas and along the Rio Grande.

DOVES & ALLIES

These familiar birds are common and widespread. All species coo. They feed largely on seeds, grain and insects.

ROCK PIGEON
Columba livia

Size: To 13 in. (33 cm)
Description: The familiar bird is typically blue-gray, although white, tan and brown variants also exist. Rump is white.
Habitat: Common in cities, towns and farmlands.
Comments: Commonly referred to as a pigeon, this introduced species is gregarious and can be trained for homing.

WHITE-WINGED DOVE
Zenaida asiatica

Size: 10–13 in. (25–33 cm)
Description: Drab brown dove told at a glance by its prominent white wing patches.
Habitat: Deserts, open woodlands.
Comments: Fast fliers, they are popular game birds.

EURASIAN COLLARED-DOVE
Streptopelia decaocto

Size: To 11 in. (28 cm)
Description: Pale beige to gray bird has a black collar on its nape.
Habitat: Open agricultural, suburban and coastal areas.
Comments: An invasive species in Texas, it was accidentally introduced to the Bahamas, spread to Florida in the 1980s and has now spread to most of the continental U.S.

MOURNING DOVE
Zenaida macroura

Size: To 13 in. (33 cm)
Description: Slender tawny bird with a relatively long neck, small head and a long, pointed tail.
Habitat: Open woodlands, suburbs.
Comments: Named for its mournful, cooing song; most frequently heard in the early morning. It feeds on the ground in flocks and bobs its head back and forth when walking. Its wings whistle loudly in flight.

INCA DOVE
Columbina inca

Size: To 8 in. (20 cm)
Description: Small dove has scaly plumage and a long tail.
Habitat: Towns, savannas, thickets, agricultural areas.
Comments: Call is a melodious – *hoo-hoo* – repeated up to 30 times a minute.

OWLS

These square-shaped birds of prey have large heads, large eyes and hooked bills. Large flattened areas around each eye form 'facial disks', which help to amplify sound toward external ear flaps. Primarily nocturnal. Sexes are similar.

BARRED OWL
Strix varia

Size: To 20 in. (50 cm)
Description: Large, stocky red-gray owl has crossbanding on its neck and breast and streaks on its belly. Lacks ear tufts.
Habitat: Mixed woodlands and swampy forests.
Comments: Call is the distinctive – *who cooks, who cooks for you all?*

GREAT HORNED OWL
Bubo virginianus

Size: 20–25 in. (50–63 cm)
Description: Large, dark brown bird with heavily barred plumage, ear tufts, yellow eyes and a white throat.
Habitat: Forests, deserts and urban areas.
Comments: Primarily nocturnal, it feeds on small mammals and birds. Sometimes spotted hunting during the day. Call is a deep, resonant – *hoo-HOO-hoooo.*

BURROWING OWL
Athene cunicularia

Size: To 11 in. (28 cm)
Description: Small terrestrial owl is told at a glance by its long legs and yellow eyes.
Habitat: Grassy fields, open plains, dry pastures, airports.
Comments: Lives in underground burrows and often nests in small colonies. The other small Texas owl, the eastern screech owl (*Megascops asio*), has yellow eyes and prominent ear tufts.

Eastern Screech Owl

WOODPECKERS

These strong-billed birds are usually spotted on tree trunks chipping away bark in search of insects or excavating nesting sites. All have stiff tails that serve as props as they forage. In spring, males drum on dead limbs and other resonant objects (e.g., garbage cans, drainpipes) to establish their territories.

RED-BELLIED WOODPECKER
Melanerpes carolinus
Size: To 11 in. (28 cm)

Description: Robin-sized woodpecker with a black and white striped back. Male has a red cap and nape; female has a red nape only. Reddish belly patch is seldom visible.

Habitat: Deciduous and mixed woods, backyards.

Comments: The most common and conspicuous woodpecker in eastern Texas.

GOLDEN-FRONTED WOODPECKER
Melanerpes aurifrons
Size: To 10 in. (25 cm)

Description: Brownish bird with barred, black and white back and wings.

Habitat: Dry woodlands, mesquite brushlands.

Comments: Permanent resident of north-central Texas through the Edwards Plateau and south Texas.

YELLOW-BELLIED SAPSUCKER
Sphyrapicus varius
Size: To 9 in. (23 cm)

Description: Note red forehead, throat, black and white facial pattern and creamy yellow belly.

Habitat: Deciduous and mixed forests statewide in winter.

Comments: Drills holes in trees and feeds on the sap and insects that collect there.

PILEATED WOODPECKER
Dryocopus pileatus
Size: To 17 in. (43 cm)

Description: Large black woodpecker distinguished by its prominent red head crest and white neck stripes.

Habitat: Forests in eastern one third of Texas.

Comments: Often detected by the slow, rhythmic hammering noise it makes excavating cavities in trees.

NORTHERN FLICKER
Colaptes auratus
Size: To 13 in. (33 cm)

Description: Brown, jay-sized bird with barred back, spotted breast and black bib. Wing and tail linings are yellow. Male has a black mustache.

Habitat: Woodlands, open areas, suburbs.

Comments: Commonly forages on the ground in search of insects and invertebrates.

RED-HEADED WOODPECKER
Melanerpes erythrocephalus
Size: To 10 in. (25 cm)

Description: Striking black and white bird has a bright scarlet head.

Habitat: Mature woodlands, open country.

Comments: Found in open agricultural areas like orchards that have groves of dead or dying trees.

DOWNY WOODPECKER
Picoides pubescens
Size: To 6 in. (15 cm)

Description: A small, sparrow-sized, black and white woodpecker with a small bill. Males have a small red head patch.

Habitat: Wooded areas.

Comments: Common resident is often seen at feeders in winter. The similar, hairy woodpecker (*P. villosus*; 10 in./25 cm) is larger and has a longer bill.

Hairy Woodpecker

LADDER-BACKED WOODPECKER
Picoides scalaris
Size: To 7 in. (18 cm)

Description: Distinguished by its strongly barred black and white back. Facial pattern forms a triangle of white on cheek. Male has a red cap, female has a black cap.

Habitat: Dry woodlands.

Comments: Frequents ranches and parks in rural areas.

CUCKOOS & ALLIES

Slender birds have rounded wings and a curved beak.

GREATER ROADRUNNER
Geococcyx californianus
Size: 20–24 in. (50–60 cm)

Description: Long-legged, gray-brown bird with a crested head and long tail.

Habitat: Open areas in habitats including deserts and oak woodlands.

Comments: A ground-dwelling bird, it can maintain speeds of 15 mph (24 kph) while running. Feeds on small mammals, snakes and insects. Often spotted darting across desert roads after prey.

YELLOW-BILLED CUCKOO
Coccyzus americanus
Size: To 14 in. (35 cm)

Description: Thin, streamlined bird has a long, graduated tail. Plumage is brown above and white below. Narrow tail is distinctively striped on the underside.

Habitat: Forests, gardens.

Black-billed Cuckoo

Comments: Call is a repetitive – *ka-ka-ka-koup-koup-koup*. The similar black-billed cuckoo (*C. erythropthalmus*) is found in the eastern third of Texas.

PARROTS & ALLIES

Slender birds have rounded wings and curved beaks.

MONK PARAKEET
Myiopsitta monachus
Size: To 11.5 in. (29 cm)

Description: This small bright green parrot has a grayish breast and bright yellow-gray belly.

Habitat: Towns, agricultural areas, open woodlands.

Comments: An introduced species, it has established populations in Dallas, Fort Worth, Austin and Houston. Builds large colonial nests on trees and poles. The all-black, parrot-like groove-billed ani (*Crotophaga sulcirostris*) is a common summer resident along the southern and central coastal plain.

Groove-billed Ani

FLYCATCHERS

These compact birds characteristically sit on exposed perches and dart out to capture passing insects.

EASTERN PHOEBE
Sayornis phoebe
Size: To 7 in. (18 cm)

Description: Brownish gray above and whitish with a pale olive wash on sides below.

Habitat: Woodlands, farmlands and suburbs near water.

Comments: Call is two whistled notes resembling – *fee-bee* – accented on the first syllable.

VERMILLION FLYCATCHER
Pyrocephalus rubinus
Size: To 6 in. (15 cm)

Description: Male has a brilliant scarlet crown and underparts and dark brown back. Female is brownish with underpart streaked in pink to yellow to white.

Habitat: Trees and shrubs along waterways and roadsides.

Comments: Is conspicuous in southern Texas near homes and farmyards.

SCISSOR-TAILED FLYCATCHER
Tyrannus forficatus
Size: To 13 in. (33 cm)

Description: Pearly gray above and white below with an orange-buff belly. Armpits are salmon-colored. Females have shorter tails than the males.

Habitat: Semi-open areas.

Comments: Also known as the Texas bird-of-paradise and swallow-tailed flycatcher. Typically nests in isolated trees and shrubs and feeds on insects and berries in summer. Winters in Mexico and Central America.

MOCKINGBIRDS & THRASHERS

These long-tailed birds with long, down-turned bills sing loud repetitious songs.

BROWN THRASHER
Toxostoma rufum

Size: To 12 in. (30 cm)

Description: Rich brown above and heavily streaked below, it is distinguished by its long tail and slightly decurved bill.

Habitat: Edges of woodlands and thickets, city parks, farmlands.

Comments: Song is a series of squeaky phrases of warbles, each repeated twice.

NORTHERN MOCKINGBIRD
Mimus polyglottos

Size: 9–11 in. (23–28 cm)

Description: Slender, long-tailed bird with gray back and light underparts. Wings flash white in flight.

Habitat: Woodlands, urban parks and gardens.

Comments: A superb singer that is named for its habit of mimicking ambient sounds ranging from the calls of other birds to traffic noises. Often flicks its tail from side to side while perching.

Texas' State Bird

CHICKADEES & ALLIES

Small, friendly birds with short bills and long tails that occur in small flocks. Common at feeders.

CAROLINA CHICKADEE
Poecile carolinensis

Size: To 5 in. (13 cm)

Description: Identified by its small size, fluffy gray plumage, black cap and bib and white face patch.

Habitat: Deciduous woods, urban areas.

Comments: Very active and inquisitive, it is easily attracted to feeders and tame enough to be fed by hand. Name-saying call is a clear – *chick-a-dee-dee-dee*.

BLACK-CRESTED TITMOUSE
Baeolophus atricristatus

Size: To 6 in. (15 cm)

Description: Distinguished by its black crest and white forehead.

Habitat: Woodlands, canyons, towns.

Comments: Call a sharp, whistled – *peter, peter, peter* – with the notes slightly higher than the tufted titmouse.

TUFTED TITMOUSE
Baeolophus bicolor
Size: To 6 in. (15 cm)

Description: Gray above, light below with buff sides, gray crest and black forehead.

Habitat: Moist deciduous woodlands, city parks.

Comments: A highly social bird, it is common at feeders in winter. Typical song is a loud, whistled – *peter, peter, peter*.

GNATCATCHERS & KINGLETS

Tiny, active olive to gray woodland birds.

BLUE-GRAY GNATCATCHER
Polioptila caerulea
Size: To 5 in. (13 cm)

Description: Tiny, slender, long-tailed, blue-gray bird has white undersides and a white eye ring.

Habitat: Deciduous woodlands, streamside thickets, pinyon-juniper and oak woodlands.

Comments: Lively birds often flick their long tails when gleaning insects from trees and shrubs.

RUBY-CROWNED KINGLET
Regulus calendula
Size: To 4 in. (10 cm)

Description: Very small bird has white wing bars, a broken white eye ring and a scarlet crown. Male's crown patch is often concealed.

Habitat: Coniferous forests in summer, deciduous woodlands in winter.

Comments: Song is an excited musical chattering. Scolding call is a two-note – *chit-dit*. It often flicks its wings when foraging for insects.

SWALLOWS

These acrobatic fliers have short bills, long, pointed wings and long tails (often forked). Their wide mouths are adapted for scooping up insects on the wing.

CLIFF SWALLOW
Petrochelidon pyrrhonota
Size: To 6 in. (15 cm)
Description: Small square-tailed blue and rufous bird with a buff rump.
Habitat: Open areas near water and a mud source.
Comments: Builds gourd-shaped nests of mud that stick to cliffs and buildings.

PURPLE MARTIN
Progne subis
Size: To 8 in. (20 cm)
Description: Distinguished by its purple-black plumage and slightly forked tail.
Habitat: Wooded areas in cities and towns.
Comments: Frequently glides in circles when flying. Nests in colonies, and is easily attracted to multi-celled bird houses. Most common between January and July.

BARN SWALLOW
Hirundo rustica
Size: 6–8 in. (15–20 cm)
Description: Blue-black above, cinnamon below, it is easily identified in flight by its long, forked tail.
Habitat: Open woods, fields, farms and lakes.
Comments: Commonly nests in building eaves and under bridges. The similar cliff swallow (*Petrochelidon pyrrhonota*) has a square-edged tail.

VIREOS

Plainly colored, sluggish birds glean insects from the foliage of trees. Many have eye rings.

WHITE-EYED VIREO
Vireo griseus
Size: To 5 in. (13 cm)
Description: Greenish above and white below with yellow flanks, yellow "spectacle" and white eyes.
Habitat: Swampy thickets, bushy hillsides with tangled shrubs.
Comments: An avid singer, its songs typically are 5–7 loud notes slurred together that begin and end with an emphatic chirp.

NUTHATCHES

Nuthatches are stout little birds with thin, sharp bills and stumpy tails.

WHITE-BREASTED NUTHATCH
Sitta carolinensis
Size: 5–6 in. (13–15 cm)
Description: Chunky, white-faced, grayish bird has a black cap, white underparts and short, sharp bill.
Habitat: Coniferous forests, pine-oak woodlands.
Comments: Creeps about on tree trunks and branches searching for insects, often descending head first.

WRENS

This family of birds has the distinctive habit of cocking its tails in the air when perching.

CAROLINA WREN
Thyrothorus ludovicianus
Size: To 6 in. (15 cm)
Description: Brown above, buff colored below with a white throat and white eye stripe.
Habitat: Thickets, brushy areas, ravines, towns.
Comments: Often nests in man-made containers including flower pots. Call is a loud, whistled – *teakettle-teakettle-teakettle* or *cheery-cheery-cheery*.

BEWICK'S WREN
Thryomanes bewickii
Size: To 5.25 in. (13 cm)
Description: Gray to red-gray bird has a white eye stripe and a long striped tail.
Habitat: Thickets, fencerows, open woodlands.
Comments: Loud melodious song is 2–5 notes followed by a trill.

VERDINS

Small, plump birds that often travel in small flocks.

VERDIN
Auriparus flaviceps
Size: 3–5 in. (8–13 cm)
Description: Small grayish bird with a yellow head and chestnut shoulders. Note long tail and sharply pointed bill.
Habitat: Dry brushy and shrubby areas.
Comments: Unusual nest consists of a ball of dried vegetation with a hole in the side. Feeds on insects, berries and seeds.

CROWS & ALLIES

These large, omnivorous birds are very common. Most have stout bills with bristles near the base. Sexes are similar.

WOODHOUSE'S SCRUB JAY
Aphelocoma woodhouseii

Size: To 13 in. (33 cm)

Description: A streamlined blue bird with a long bill and tail. Key field marks are white throat, incomplete blue necklace and brown back.

Habitat: Oak-chaparral, pinyon-juniper woodlands in western Texas.

Comments: Common in cities and towns. Flight is undulating and short, followed by a sweeping glide.

AMERICAN CROW
Corvus brachyrhynchos

Size: To 18 in. (45 cm)

Description: Told by black plumage and thick black bill. Call is a distinct – *caw*.

Habitat: Rural and wilderness areas.

Comments: Eats everything from insects and grain to small birds and refuse. The similar, slightly smaller, fish crow (*C. ossifragus*; 20 in./50 cm) is more common in coastal and urban areas. Its call is a nasal – *uh, uh*.

CHIHUAHUAN RAVEN
Corvus cryptoleucus

Size: To 20 in. (50 cm)

Description: A large black bird with a heavy bill, wedge-shaped tail and shaggy head and throat feathers.

Habitat: Deserts, scrubby grasslands, farmlands in western Texas.

Common Raven

Comments: Distinguished from crows by its low, croaking call. Feeds primarily on insects, small animals and carrion. The larger common raven (*C. corax*), also found in mountains and deserts in western Texas, is up to 30 in. (75 cm) long.

BLUE JAY
Cyanocitta cristata
Size: To 14 in. (35 cm)
Description: Easily recognized by its crested head, blue back and black neckband.
Habitat: Woodlands and open areas.
Comments: Widespread throughout Texas, it is a bold, aggressive bird that often dominates backyard feeders. It has several vocalizations, some of which are quite musical. Call is a piercing – *jay-jay-jay*!

GREEN JAY
Cyanocorax yncas
Size: To 14 in. (35 cm)
Description: Unmistakable jay is bright green above, yellow below and has a blue head and a green throat.
Habitat: Riparian and thorn forests, savanna.
Comments: Tropical species is common in the southern tip of Texas.

SHRIKES

Shrikes feed on insects, small birds and rodents. Nicknamed butcher birds, they will cache excess food taken when hunting by impaling it on tree thorns or barbed wire.

LOGGERHEAD SHRIKE
Lanius ludovicianus
Size: 8–10 in. (20–25 cm)
Description: Gray-backed bird with a black mask and a stout, hooked bill.
Habitat: Forests and open areas including deserts and grasslands.
Comments: Flight is undulating. Often seen perching atop trees and telephone wires in open country.

STARLINGS

Introduced from Europe, they are abundant in cities and towns.

EUROPEAN STARLING
Sturnus vulgaris
Size: To 8 in. (20 cm)
Description: Chubby bird with a yellow bill and a short tail. In winter, the plumage becomes brightly flecked and the bill darkens.
Habitat: Fields, cities.
Comments: This invasive species was introduced from England in the 1890s. Today, over 200 million birds are blamed for $800 million in agricultural losses annually. Highly aggressive, they outcompete native species for food and nesting sites.

THRUSHES

This group of woodland birds includes many good singers. Sexes are similar in most.

EASTERN BLUEBIRD
Sialia sialis
Size: To 7 in. (18 cm)
Description: Blue above, brick red below with a white belly. Females are blue-gray above, gray-white below.
Habitat: Open woodlands, meadows, grasslands, farms.
Comments: Song is a melodious warbling whistle – *tu-wheet-tudu*. Call is a musical – *turee* or *queedle*.

♀

♂

AMERICAN ROBIN
Turdus migratorius
Size: To 11 in. (28 cm)
Description: Gray above and bright red below, it has a black head and white throat streaks.
Habitat: Towns, fields, parklands, open woodlands.
Comments: Forages on the ground for insects, snails and worms. Most abundant in spring and fall. Song is a melodious series of rising and falling notes – *cheer-up, cheerily, cheer-up, cheery*.

HERMIT THRUSH
Catharus guttatus
Size: To 7 in. (18 cm)
Description: Brown-gray bird has a heavily spotted breast and a long, rufous tail.
Habitat: Coniferous and mixed forests.
Comments: Song starts with a whistle, followed by 3–4 phrases of notes at different pitches.

WAXWINGS

These gregarious birds are named for their red wing marks that look like waxy droplets.

CEDAR WAXWING
Bombycilla cedrorum
Size: 6–8 in. (15–20 cm)
Description: Told at a glance by its sleek, crested head, yellow belly, yellow-tipped tail and red wing marks.
Habitat: Open deciduous woods, orchards, urban areas.
Comments: Diet consists largely of berries and insects. Occurs in small flocks.

WARBLERS & ALLIES

Members of this large family of highly active, insect-eating birds are distinguished from other small birds by their thin, pointed bills. Males tend to be more brightly colored than females and are the only singers. Those that are migrants tend to be duller-colored than shown here.

YELLOW-RUMPED WARBLER
Setophaga coronata
Size: To 6 in. (15 cm)

Description: Blue gray above, it has a yellow cap, rump and wing patches. Two races exist. The Myrtle race has a white throat and the Audubon's race has a yellow throat.

Habitat: Forested and open areas.

Comments: Vivid and conspicuous when foraging, it sings from tree canopies.

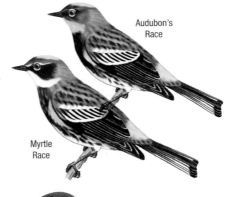

Audubon's Race

Myrtle Race

YELLOW-BREASTED CHAT
Icteria virens
Size: To 7 in. (18 cm)

Description: Large warbler is olive-brown above, yellow below and has conspicuous white spectacles and a long tail.

Habitat: Dense thickets, brushy pastures statewide.

Comments: When flying, it will often hover with its feet dangling.

COMMON YELLOWTHROAT
Geothlypis trichas
Size: To 5 in. (13 cm)

Description: Olive green above, yellow below with a white-bordered black mask. Females are dull yellow below and lack the mask.

Habitat: Moist, grassy areas, marshes, thickets.

Comments: A year-round resident, it is abundant and widespread throughout the state.

ORANGE-CROWNED WARBLER
Oreothlypis celata
Size: 4–5.5 in. (11–14 cm)

Description: Drab olive bird with yellowish underparts and an orange crown patch that is often hidden. Olive-yellow underparts are faintly streaked.

Habitat: Open woodland, brushy areas.

Comments: Orange crown patch is often concealed. Song is a fast trill changing in pitch going up or down the scale.

BLACKBIRDS & ALLIES

A diverse group of birds ranging from iridescent black birds to brightly-colored meadowlarks and orioles. All have conical, sharply-pointed bills.

RED-WINGED BLACKBIRD
Agelaius phoeniceus
Size: To 9 in. (23 cm)
Description: Black male has distinctive red shoulder patches. Brown females look like large sparrows.
Habitat: Swamps, marshes and wet fields.
Comments: Usually nests in reeds or tall grass near water and is common in urban parks. Gurgling, musical song – *kon-la-REE* – is a common marsh sound.

BREWER'S BLACKBIRD
Euphagus cyanocephalus
Size: To 9 in. (23 cm)
Description: Glossy black bird has yellow eyes. Male has a purplish gloss on its head and a greenish gloss on its back. Females are brownish.
Habitat: Prairies, pastures, farmlands, parks.
Comments: Common in open habitats in urban areas. Often found near livestock.

COMMON GRACKLE
Quiscalus quiscula
Size: To 14 in. (35 cm)
Description: Black-purple bird with long, wedge-shaped tail and yellow eyes.
Habitat: Open woods, fields and parks statewide.
Comments: Common resident that occurs in large flocks during winter. Abundant near human dwellings. The similar, larger, boat-tailed grackle (*Q. major*) is more common in coastal areas.

EASTERN MEADOWLARK
Sturnella magna
Size: To 9 in. (23 cm)
Description: Mottled brown bird with a bright yellow breast, white-edged tail, and dark V-shaped neckband.
Habitat: Grassy fields, meadows, marshes.
Comments: Nests and forages on the ground. Loud, flute-like, gurgling song is distinctive.

GREAT-TAILED GRACKLE
Quiscalus mexicanus

Size: 16–17 in. (40–43 cm)
Description: Purplish-black bird has a
long tail shaped like a boat's keel. Eyes
are yellow. Females are brown above with
buff underparts.
Habitat: Towns, fields.
Comments: Call includes a series of whistles and
harsh creaks. Very common resident in urban areas.

ORCHARD ORIOLE
Icterus spurius

Size: To 7 in. (18 cm)
Description: Has black hood, wings and tail and
a bright chestnut belly. Females are greenish.
Habitat: Orchards, parks, gardens.
Comments: Common resident in east and
central Texas.

BROWN-HEADED COWBIRD
Molothrus ater

Size: 6–8 in. (15–20 cm)
Description: Metallic green-black bird with brown
hood and heavy bill.
Habitat: Open woods, farmlands and fields (often near
livestock) statewide.
Comments: Female is noted for her parasitic habit
of laying eggs in the nests of other birds. While some
species remove the new egg, most will raise the cowbird
as their own, often at the expense of their young.

WEAVER FINCHES

These sparrow-like birds were introduced to North America in 1850 and are now
widespread throughout the continent.

HOUSE SPARROW
Passer domesticus

Size: To 6 in. (15 cm)
Description: Black throat and brown nape of male are
diagnostic. Females and young are dull brown with a
light eye stripe.
Habitat: Very common in a variety of habitats.
Comments: Introduced from Europe, these gregarious,
social birds are common throughout Texas.

FINCHES, SPARROWS & ALLIES

Members of this family have short, thick, seed-cracking bills.

NORTHERN CARDINAL
Cardinalis cardinalis

Size: To 9 in. (23 cm)
Description: Bright, red crested bird with a black mask and a stout bill. Females and juveniles are grayish and have an orange or brown bill.
Habitat: Woodlands, gardens, parks, backyards.
Comments: Very common in cities and towns throughout the year. Easily attracted to feeders in winter. Song is a ringing whistle – *whit-chew*.

♀

♂

HOUSE FINCH
Haemorhous mexicanus

Size: 5–6 in. (13–15 cm)
Description: Brown bird with a reddish forehead, streaked breast and rump.
Habitat: Deserts, woodlands, farms and urban areas in the western two thirds of Texas.
Comments: Highly social birds, they are easily attracted to feeders and nesting sites. Call is a nasal – *wink*.

PAINTED BUNTING
Passerina ciris

Size: To 6 in. (15 cm)
Description: Gaudy male has purple head, red underparts and green wings. Females are greenish.
Habitat: Thickets, hedgerows, swampy areas, dune scrub.
Comments: Relatively common in Texas, they are rarely seen since they inhabit dense brush.

INDIGO BUNTING
Passerina cyanea

Size: To 6 in. (15 cm)
Description: Brilliant blue bird is unmistakable. Females are brownish.
Habitat: Woodlands, fields.
Comments: Males sing from exposed perches in summer. Song is a series of varied phrases.

AMERICAN GOLDFINCH
Spinus tristis
Size: To 5 in. (13 cm)

Description: Male is bright yellow with a black cap, black tail and wings and a white rump. Duller female lacks a cap.

Habitat: Wooded groves, gardens.

Comments: Often found in flocks. Can be identified on the wing by its deeply dipping-soaring flight. Canary-like song is bright and cheery.

LESSER GOLDFINCH
Spinus psaltria
Size: 4–5 in. (10–13 cm)

Description: Male has a black cap, a black or greenish back, yellow underparts and bold white wing marks. Duller female lacks a cap.

Habitat: Wooded groves, gardens, parks, brushy fields.

Comments: Often found in flocks. Song is a rapidly repeated series of ascending or descending notes.

WHITE-CROWNED SPARROW
Zonotrichia leucophrys
Size: To 7 in. (18 cm)

Description: Brown above and gray below, it has a black and white striped crown and a pinkish, orange or yellowish bill.

Habitat: Thickets and brushy areas in coniferous and deciduous woodlands.

Comments: Feeds most often on the ground. Common at feeders in winter. Song is one or more whistled notes followed with trills and buzzes.

WHITE-THROATED SPARROW
Zonotrichia albicollis
Size: To 7 in. (18 cm)

Description: Similar to the white-crowned sparrow, it has bright yellow patches in front of the eye.

Habitat: Coniferous and mixed woodlands, fencerows, swamps, weedy fields.

Comments: Usually forages on the ground. Song resembles – *Old Sam Peabody, Peabody, Peabody* or *Oh sweet Canada, Canada, Canada.*

The diverse habitats of Texas (swamps, marshes, pine forests, rocky hills, mountains, deserts, prairies) combined with its central location where species from the east, west and Mexico meet, make it one of the prime locations to find and study reptiles and amphibians. In total, there are over 225 species.

REPTILES

Reptiles can generally be described as terrestrial, scaly-skinned creatures that breathe through lungs. The majority reproduce by laying eggs on land. In some, the eggs develop inside the mother who later gives birth to live young. Contrary to popular belief, very few are harmful to man, and many are valuable in controlling rodent and insect populations. The most common types of reptiles in Texas are:

| Turtles | Lizards | Snakes | Crocodilians |

AMPHIBIANS

Amphibians are smooth-skinned, limbed vertebrates that live in moist habitats and breathe through lungs, skin, gills or a combination of all three. While many spend much of their lives on land, they still depend on a watery environment to complete their life cycle. Most reproduce by laying eggs in or near water. The young hatch as swimming larvae that breathe through gills. After a short developmental period, the larvae metamorphose into young adults with lungs and legs. The most common types of Texas amphibians are:

| Salamanders | Frogs | Toads |

How to Find Reptiles & Amphibians

Reptiles are secretive but can be observed if you know where to look. Turtles are found on the edges of ponds and lakes and often sun themselves on rocks and logs. Lizards sun themselves in habitats ranging from open deserts to suburban back yards and are the most conspicuous reptiles. Snakes can be found in deserts, canyons and along trails and watercourses. When seeking reptiles, be careful. Many snakes are well-camouflaged and can be sluggish in the morning or after eating. Do not put hands in places you can't see into. Turn over rocks and logs with a stick or tool.

Frogs are found in wet areas on or near the water. Toads are more terrestrial and may be found far from water, especially during the day. Salamanders are more secretive and rarely venture out of their cool, moist habitats.

TURTLES

Turtles are reptiles that have a bony or leathery shell, four limbs and a tail. The top of the shell (carapace) protects the back and sides, and the lower shell (plastron) protects the underbelly. The head can be fully or partially withdrawn into the shell. The main groups include: **1. Freshwater Turtles:** aquatic and semi-aquatic species with smooth shells, webbed feet and streamlined shells; **2. Terrestrial Turtles:** primarily land-dwelling with prominent limbs, club-shaped feet and high-domed shells; and **3. Sea Turtles:** large species live in the open ocean and have limbs adapted as flippers.

SNAPPING TURTLE
Chelydra serpentina
Size: To 18 in. (45 cm)

Description: Distinguished by its rough, knobby shell and long tail that is saw-toothed on its upper edge.

Habitat: Ponds and lakes with muddy bottoms and abundant vegetation.

Comments: An aggressive predator, it feeds on fishes, amphibians, reptiles, mammals and birds. It should be treated with caution when encountered on land as it will often lunge at humans and can inflict serious cuts. The huge alligator snapping turtle (*Macrochelys temminckii*) weighs up to 300 lbs. (135 kg) and is found in the eastern quarter of Texas.

Alligator Snapping Turtle

TEXAS MAP TURTLE
Graptemys versa
Size: To 8 in. (20 cm)

Description: Distinguished by projecting, convex scutes on back of carapace. Note light, orange to yellow J-shaped line behind eye.

Habitat: Fast waters of the Colorado River System in central Texas.

Comments: Named for the fine lines on its carapace that create map-like images.

YELLOW MUD TURTLE
Kinosternon flavescens
Size: To 6 in. (15 cm)

Description: Small turtle has yellow areas on its throat, head and neck.

Habitat: Found in a variety of wet habitats with muddy bottoms throughout most of Texas.

Comments: In the drier west, it can be found in drainage ditches, cattle tanks and sewer drains. Primarily carnivorous, it feeds on fish, insects, crayfish/snails, amphibians and even carrion. The Mississippi Mud Turtle (*K. subrubrum hippocrepis*) found in eastern Texas is easily distinguished by the two light lines on its head.

Mississippi Mud Turtle

SMOOTH SOFTSHELL
Apalone mutica
Size: To 20 in. (50 cm)
Description: Periscope-like snout is distinctive. Smooth, leathery shell lacks bumps or projections.
Habitat: Aquatic habitats in east Texas.
Comments: Noted for its habit of staying completely submerged with only the tip of its nose poking out of the water. Heavily harvested for food, it is a species of special concern. The similar Texas spiny softshell (*A. spinifera*) has a shell with small spines and a rough, sandpaper-like texture.

Texas Spiny Softshell

RED-EARED SLIDER
Trachemys scripta elegans
Size: To 11 in. (28 cm)
Description: Greenish turtle is easily recognized by its red ear patch.
Habitat: Found in quiet, well-vegetated waters with muddy bottoms.
Comments: The most popular pet turtle in the U.S., many wild populations are a result of pet releases.

TEXAS RIVER COOTER
Pseudemys texana
Size: To 12 in. (30 cm)
Description: Olive to black carapace has alternating yellow lines. Note broad head markings. Underside is yellowish.
Habitat: Creeks, rivers, ditches and lakes in east and central Texas.
Comments: Also known as Texas slider, it is found in the river basins of the Brazos, Guadalupe, Colorado and San Antonio rivers.

WESTERN CHICKEN TURTLE
Deirochelys reticularia miaria
Size: To 10 in. (25 cm)
Description: Note long striped neck and striped legs. Shell has a light net-like pattern.
Habitat: Shallow waters and drainage ditches in the eastern quarter of Texas.
Comments: An omnivor, it eats crayfish, fish, fruit, invertebrates and plants. The common name refers to the taste of its meat.

TEXAS DIAMONDBACK TERRAPIN
Malaclemys terrapin litoralis
Size: To 9 in. (23 cm)

Description: Dark turtle is distinguished by its sculpted carapace where the scutes have deep growth rings.

Habitat: Lives in coastal brackish habitats (never in open ocean).

Comments: Feeds on fish, insects, carrion and aquatic invertebrates. Loss of habitat and hunting (flesh was considered a delicacy) are the main threats to this species.

ORNATE BOX TURTLE
Terrapene ornata
Size: To 5 in. (13 cm)

Description: Domed carapace has radiating light lines and is flattened on the top. Lines are often broken into spots.

Habitat: Open areas including pastures, prairies and open woodlands.

Comments: Unlike many turtles, the box turtle has hinged plastrons that allow it to retract its head, neck and limbs completely into its shell. Feeds primarily on insects, slugs, snails, carrion and plants.

Underside of box turtle with shell closed.

TEXAS TORTOISE
Gopherus berlandieri
Size: To 14 in. (35 cm)

Description: Domed, tan-yellow-orange carapace has deep ridges. Legs are thick and columnar.

Habitat: Dry sandy areas of southern Texas.

Comments: Feeds on vegetation and the pads, fruits and flowers of the prickly pear cactus and other succulents. Unlike other tortoises, it is not an adept burrower.

KEMP'S RIDLEY SEA TURTLE
Lepidochelys kempii
Size: 24–28 in. (60–70 cm)

Description: Circular carapace is olive-gray-green above and yellowish below. Flippers are dark-spotted.

Habitat: Open ocean and Gulf waters.

Comments: The most endangered sea turtle in the world, it nests on Texas beaches April–July. It is the only sea turtle that nests primarily during the day. The loggerhead sea turtles (*Caretta caretta*) are occasional visitors to Texas and much less frequent nesters.

Texas' State Sea Turtle

Loggerhead Sea Turtle

CROCODILIANS

Large reptiles have armor-plated skin and huge, toothy jaws. All are aquatic carnivores that feed on fish and other animals. Only the American Alligator and American Crocodile are native to the U.S. All are dangerous to humans.

AMERICAN ALLIGATOR
Alligator mississippiensis

Size: To 19 ft. (5.7 m)

Description: Distinguished by its broad, rounded snout and blackish color. When jaws are closed, only upper teeth are visible.

Habitat: Freshwater lakes, waterways, marshes and swamps.

Comments: During droughts, the alligator excavates a pool (gator hole) in marshes, which is beneficial to many forms of wildlife. During cooler months, it hibernates in dens along the banks of waterways and lakes.

LIZARDS

Lizards are scaly-skinned animals that usually have 4 legs and a tail, movable eyelids, visible ear openings, claws and toothed jaws. A few species are legless and superficially resemble snakes. Lizards represent the largest group of living reptiles and range in size from tiny skinks to the giant 10-foot-long monitor lizards of Indonesia. Of the more than 3,000 species found worldwide, 95 occur in the U.S.

GREEN ANOLE
Anolis carolinensis

Size: To 8 in. (20 cm)

Description: Slender green lizard with a long, wedge-shaped snout and a pink or gray throat fan (dewlap). Able to change color from green to brown to match surroundings of leaves or bark.

Habitat: Variable, including forests, swamps and urban areas.

Comments: The brown (Cuban) anole (*A. sagrei*) is established in isolated areas of southeast Texas. Male may have a crest or ridge along midline.

WESTERN WHIPTAIL
Aspidoscelis tigris

Size: To 12 in. (30 cm)

Description: A gray, yellowish or brown lizard with bars, spots or a web of lines on its back and sides. Note its long tail.

Habitat: Deserts and open forests.

Comments: Active during the day and often encountered. Moves in jerky steps, with its head darting side-to-side.

GREAT PLAINS SKINK
Plestiodon obsoletus

Size: To 14 in. (35 cm)

Description: Olive-brown to tan lizard has yellowish underside.

Habitat: Grasslands with soil suitable for burrowing in all but eastern Texas.

Comments: The largest skink in Texas. The little brown skink (*Scincella lateralis*) is the smallest skink in Texas and measures a mere 5 in. (13 cm). It is found in eastern and southern Texas.

Little Brown Skink

TEXAS EARLESS LIZARD
Cophosaurus texanus texanus

Size: To 7 in. (18 cm)

Description: Note black-striped tail and yellow and brown stripes near the groin.

Habitat: Desert flats and streambeds in the western two thirds of the state.

Comments: Highly active, it darts around during the day with its tail elevated.

COLLARED LIZARD
Crotaphytus collaris

Size: 9–14 in. (23–35 cm)

Description: Greenish, long-tailed lizard with two dark collar markings.

Habitat: Rocky areas in deserts and foothills.

Comments: It flees danger by running swiftly on its hind legs. Will bite readily if handled.

TEXAS BANDED GECKO
Coleonyx brevis

Size: To 5 in. (13 cm)

Description: Brownish lizard has light yellow crossbands.

Habitat: Rocky areas in east and south Texas.

Comments: Nocturnal species is often seen along roadways at night foraging for insects.

TEXAS HORNED LIZARD
Phrynosoma cornutum

Size: 2.5–7 in. (6–18 cm)

Description: Flattened, broad lizard has spines down both sides and two on the head that resemble horns.

Habitat: Sandy areas with little vegetation.

Comments: Usually seen at dawn and dusk feeding on ants, it is considered a threatened species.

Texas' State Reptile

TEXAS SPINY LIZARD
Sceloporus olivaceus
Size: To 11 in. (28 cm)
Description: Large red-brown lizard has long toes and large, spiny dorsal scales.
Habitat: Usually seen in trees including mesquite, oak, cottonwood and cedar.
Comments: Diurnal species is very adept at climbing and is well-camouflaged on tree trunks and limbs.

SLENDER GLASS LIZARD
Ophisaurus attenuatus
Size: 22–42 in. (55–105 cm)
Description: Pale yellow, legless lizard has a dark mid-dorsal stripe.
Habitat: Grasslands, wooded areas.
Comments: When threatened, it may "shatter" into several pieces leaving its tail behind (which will regrow over time).

SNAKES

Snakes are limbless reptiles with dry, scaly skin, toothed jaws, no ear openings or eyelids and a single row of belly scales. They move by contracting their muscles in waves and undulating over the ground. All are carnivorous and swallow their prey whole. They flick their tongues in and out constantly to 'taste' and 'smell' the air around them. Most continue to grow in length during their life and shed their outer skin periodically. Of the over 100 snake species found in Texas, only 15 are venomous.

BULL SNAKE
Pituophis catenifer sayi
Size: To 72 in. (1.8 m)
Description: Yellowish snake has dark black, brown or reddish blotches. Note dark blotch extending from the eye to the jaw.
Habitat: Prairies, deserts, farms.

Comments: Commonly encountered, it feeds primarily on rodents and is valued for controlling the spread of mice.

EASTERN YELLOW-BELLIED RACER
Coluber constrictor flaviventris
Size: To 50 in. (1.25 m)
Description: Dorsal color is variable, ranging from brown, gray and olive to dull green and dark blue. Distinguished by yellow belly.
Habitat: Open areas with underbrush.

Comments: One of five species of *Coluber constrictor* found in Texas, it is active during the day and often encountered.

GREAT PLAINS RAT SNAKE
Pantherophis guttata emoryi

Size: To 3 ft. (90 cm)
Description: Gray snake is covered in brown blotches. Neck lines form a spearpoint on the head.
Habitat: Rocky hillsides, canyons, wooded areas.
Comments: Also called brown rat snake and chicken snake.

TEXAS RAT SNAKE
Elaphe obsoleta lindheimeri

Size: To 6 ft. (1.8 m)
Description: Gray to yellowish snake is covered in dark blotches. Head is often black.
Habitat: Bayous, swamps, woodlands.
Comments: An excellent climber, it is often seen in trees.

DESERT KINGSNAKE
Lampropeltis getula splendida

Size: To 45 in. (1.1 m)
Description: Brown to black snake it has dark blotches down back and sides speckled with white to yellowish dots.
Habitat: Inhabits dry areas and is often found near water.
Comments: Immune to rattlesnake venom, it commonly feeds on rattlesnake.

WESTERN COACHWHIP
Masticophis flagellum testaceus

Size: To 5 ft. (1.5 m)
Description: Slim, long-tailed, large-eyed snake may be reddish or brownish in different parts of its range. Tail looks like a braided whip.
Habitat: Grasslands, deserts, swamps.
Comments: Active during the day, it feeds on lizards and other snakes, rabbits and birds.

MEXICAN MILK SNAKE
Lampropeltis triangulum annulata

Size: To 30 in. (75 cm)
Description: Snake has yellow, black and red rings and a black snout.
Habitat: Wet and dry areas near water.
Comments: One of four subspecies of milk snake found in Texas, its name refers to the myth of how it obtains nourishment by suckling cattle.

TEXAS CORAL SNAKE
Micrurus tener

Size: To 40 in. (1 m)

Description: Note black snout, red and yellow rings touch each other.

Habitat: Lowland areas, rocky hillsides and canyons.

Comments: Several harmless species mimic this venomous snake. The mnemonic to remember is 'Red on yellow can kill a fellow'.

WESTERN DIAMONDBACK RATTLESNAKE
Crotalus atrox

Size: 3–7 ft. (.9–2.1 m)

Description: A thick-bodied grayish snake with brown diamond-like blotches down its back. Also has distinct black-and-white bands on its tail preceding the rattle.

Habitat: Variable, from the desert to the mountains.

Comments: A very dangerous snake, its bite can be fatal to humans. One of 8 species of rattlesnake found in Texas.

COPPERHEAD
Agkistrodon contortrix

Southern Copperhead

Size: To 52 in. (1.3 m)

Description: Several variants exist in the state. The southern copperhead found in eastern Texas has hourglass markings on its back. The broad-banded copperhead found in central Texas has broad bands down its back.

Broad-banded Copperhead

Habitat: Wooded hillsides, swamp edges.

Comments: An upland version of its aquatic cousin the cottonmouth. Venomous.

COTTONMOUTH
Agkistrodon piscivorus

Size: To 5 ft. (1.5 m)

Description: Large water snake has a spade-shaped head and vertical pupils. Color is typically dark brown or black with little cross-banding. Young are brightly marked but banding and facial stripes disappear as it ages.

Habitat: Flooded woodlands, lakes, swamps, bayous, rivers, streams.

Comments: Bite is very venomous. When disturbed, it gapes widely and displays the whitish inside of its mouth. Also called water moccasin and gapper, it swims with its head held out of the water.

FROGS & TOADS

Frogs and toads are squat amphibians common near freshwater. Toads are more terrestrial than the aquatic frogs. All have large heads, large eyes, long hind legs and long, sticky tongues that they use to catch insects. Most have well-developed ears and strong voices. Only males are vocal.

BLANCHARD'S CRICKET FROG

Acris blanchardi

Size: To 3.5 in. (9 cm)

Description: Small frog with long snout has dark bars on its hind limbs and a dark backward-pointing triangle between its eyes.

Habitat: Shallow ponds and creeks.

Comments: Voice sounds like the clicking of pebbles in rapid succession.

GREEN TREEFROG

Hyla cinerea

Size: To 2.5 in. (6 cm)

Description: Small, bright green frog often has light lateral stripes. Note large toepads.

Habitat: Swamps, edges of lakes and waterways in the eastern third of the state.

Comments: Call is a cowbell-like – *quenk, quenk, quenk* – that is usually heard during damp weather.

BULLFROG

Lithobates catesbeianus

Size: To 8 in. (20 cm)

Description: Large, green-brown frog with large ear openings and a rounded snout.

Habitat: Ponds and lakes with ample vegetation throughout Texas.

Comments: Primarily nocturnal, it is often seen along shorelines. Call is a deep-pitched – *jurrrooom*. A voracious predator, it will eat anything it can swallow.

SOUTHERN LEOPARD FROG

Lithobates sphenocephalus

Size: To 5 in. (13 cm)

Description: Green to brown frog has dark-spotted back and two light dorsal ridges. Note small yellow spot in center of tympanum (eardrum).

Habitat: Margins of waterways and ponds, wet fields.

Comments: A common frog noted for its leaping ability. Also called grass frog. Call is a series of short croaks.

Toads can be distinguished from frogs by their dry, warty skin and prominent glands behind their eyes (parotoids). Some also have swellings between their eyes (bosses). When handled roughly by would-be predators, the warts and glands secrete a poisonous substance, which makes the toads extremely unpalatable. Contrary to popular belief, handling toads does not cause warts.

GULF COAST TOAD
Bufo nebulifer

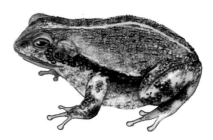

Size: To 5 in. (13 cm)
Description: Brownish to black toad has broad, dark lateral stripes and a light dorsal stripe.
Habitat: Coastal prairies and sandy beaches to irrigation ditches and suburban backyards in central and southern Texas.
Comments: Call that sounds like a wooden rattle is a short trill repeated every 1-4 seconds.

GREEN TOAD
Bufo debilis

Size: To 5.5 in. (14 cm)
Description: Flat green toad has warty skin and a net-like pattern on its body.
Habitat: Grasslands, semi-arid plains.
Comments: Active at twilight and often forages during the day.

TEXAS TOAD
Bufo speciosus

Size: To 3.5 in. (9 cm)
Description: Rounded, gray to brown toad is covered in small warts.
Habitat: Grasslands, open woodlands, sandy areas.
Comments: Nocturnal species burrows in soft soils. Feeds on insects and other invertebrates.

Texas' State Amphibian

GREAT PLAINS NARROWMOUTH TOAD
Gastrophryne olivacea

Size: To 1.5 in. (4 cm)
Description: Small gray, tan or green, egg-shaped toad has smooth skin, a small head and a pointed snout.
Habitat: Moist areas, grasslands, rocky slopes.
Comments: Nocturnal species is a prodigious burrower.

SALAMANDERS

Salamanders are smooth-skinned, tailed creatures that lack claws and ear openings. Some have the ability to regenerate tails or limbs lost to predators. Seldom seen, they live in dark, moist habitats and are nocturnal and secretive. They are most active in the spring and fall, especially near the pools where they breed.

Fertilization in most is internal but is not accomplished by copulation. During mating, the male releases a small packet of sperm that the female brushes against and draws into her body. The packet is kept in her body until she ovulates, which may be months later. Most species lay their eggs in water. Both adults and larvae are carnivorous and feed on worms and insects and other invertebrates.

TIGER SALAMANDER
Ambystoma spp.
Size: To 14 in. (35 cm)

Description: Pattern of yellowish and dark blotches is variable.

Habitat: Wet areas throughout Texas except for the eastern quarter.

Comments: Two subspecies are found in Texas, the western tiger salamander (*A. mavortium*) and the eastern tiger salamander (*A. tigrinum*).

Western

Eastern

EASTERN NEWT
Notophthalmus viridescens
Size: To 5.5 in. (14 cm)

Description: Yellow-brown to brown adult has a vertically compressed tail and has red spots on its body that vary in number and position. The juvenile is bright red-orange and has a rounded tail.

Habitat: Ponds, lakes, quiet streams, swamps, ditches.

Comments: Aquatic adult feeds in shallow water. Land-dwelling juvenile – *red eft* – is up to 3.8 in./9 cm long.

Terrestrial (juvenile) Red Eft

SMALLMOUTH SALAMANDER
Ambystoma texanum
Size: To 7.5 in. (19 cm)

Description: Gray to black salamander has a small head and mouth. Speckled variants (common in Texas) have lichen-like markings on sides and back.

Habitat: Wet habitats in eastern Texas.

Comments: When threatened, it waves its tail from side to side. Often found in debris piles near streams and lakes.

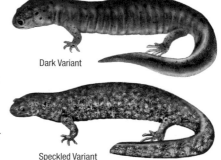

Dark Variant

Speckled Variant

Fishes are cold-blooded vertebrates that live in water and breathe dissolved oxygen through organs called gills. They are generally characterized by their size, shape, feeding habits and water temperature preference. Most live in either saltwater or freshwater, though a few species divide their lives between the two (these are referred to as anadromous fishes).

Most fishes have streamlined bodies and swim by flexing their bodies from side to side. Their fins help to steer while swimming and can also act as brakes. Many species possess an internal air bladder that acts as a depth regulator. By secreting gases into the bladder or absorbing gases from it, they are able to control the depth at which they swim.

Most fish reproduce by laying eggs freely in the water. In many, the male discharges sperm over the eggs as they are laid by the female. Depending on the species, eggs may float, sink, become attached to vegetation or be buried.

How to Identify Fishes

First, note the size, shape and color of the fish. Are there any distinguishing field marks like the double dorsal fins of the basses or the downturned lips of the suckers? Is the body thin or torpedo-shaped? Note the orientation and placement of fins on the body. Consult the text to confirm identification.

For simplicity's sake, the fishes in this guide are sorted by their habitat, rather than family, namely freshwater fishes and saltwater fishes.

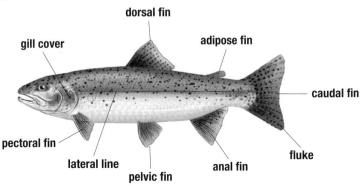

dorsal fin

gill cover · adipose fin

caudal fin

pectoral fin

lateral line · anal fin

fluke

pelvic fin

SAFELY RELEASING A FISH

A number of Texas fishes must be returned unharmed to the water if hooked. The steps to follow include:

1. Keep the fish in the water as much as possible and hold gently. Avoid squeezing.
2. Using a pair of forceps or long-nosed pliers, safely remove the hook. If the fish is hooked too deeply, cut the line as close to the hook as possible.
3. To release fish, gently hold it under the water. Point its head into the current and move it slowly backward and forward to deliver more oxygen to its gills. It will start to wriggle away when revived.

FRESHWATER FISHES

BOWFIN
Amia calva
Size: To 34 in. (85 cm)
Description: Torpedo-shaped fish has a long dorsal fin extending for more than half its total body length. Note rounded tail.
Habitat: Sluggish streams, swamps, vegetated lakes.

Comments: A transitional species, bowfins possess characteristics of both primitive and modern fishes including a skeleton that is partially composed of cartilage.

CHANNEL CATFISH
Ictalurus punctatus
Size: To 4 ft. (1.2 m)
Description: Olive to blue-gray catfish has dark spots scattered on its back and sides. Note rounded anal fin.
Habitat: Deep pools in rivers.

Comments: A popular food and game fish, it is the species most commonly raised in hatcheries. Weighs up to 58 lbs. (26 kg).

BLUE CATFISH
Ictalurus furcatus
Size: To 5.5 ft. (1.7 m)
Description: Body is blue to blue-gray above and white below. Large anal fin has a straight edge. Body lacks spots.
Habitat: Large waterways with sandy or rocky bottoms.

Comments: One of the largest North American freshwater fishes, it is a prized table fish. Weighs up to 143 lbs. (65 kg).

FLATHEAD CATFISH
Pylodictis olivaris
Size: To 53 in. (1.38 m)
Description: This dark, mottled fish is distinguished by its wide, flat head, and jutting lower jaw. The top lobe of its caudal fin is light colored.
Habitat: Lakes, creeks and reservoirs.

Comments: Popular sport and food fish is often found in nearshore waters under some form of cover. Also called yellow catfish.

SPOTTED GAR
Lepisosteus oculatus

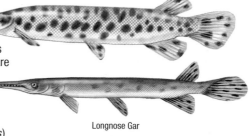

Size: To 44 in. (1.1 m)

Description: Slender, dark-spotted fish has a long, toothy snout. Dorsal and anal fins are located far back on body.

Habitat: Sluggish streams and pools with sandy or muddy bottoms.

Comments: Texas is home to four species of gar including the longnose gar (*L. osseus*) and the shortnose gar (*L. platostomus*).

Longnose Gar

Shortnose Gar

ALLIGATOR GAR
Atractosteus spatula

Size: 6–10 ft. (1.8–3 m)

Description: Large torpedo-shaped, brown to olive-colored fish has long, toothy jaws.

Habitat: Reservoirs, bayous and brackish marshes.

Comments: One of the largest freshwater fishes in North America it can weigh as much as 350 lbs. (160 kg). An ambush predator like the alligator, it floats quietly in the water before lashing out and grabbing its prey. Sought after for private aquaria, large fish may cost up to $40,000 on the black market in some countries.

GRASS CARP
Ctenopharyngodon idella

Size: 24–40 in. (.6–1 m)

Description: Robust, torpedo-shaped fish has a blunt head and a broad, short snout. Color is silvery to olive.

Habitat: Slow-moving rivers and creeks, ponds, reservoirs.

Comments: Feeds primarily on aquatic plants and is used extensively for aquatic weed control.

COMMON CARP
Cyprinus carpio

Size: To 4 ft. (1.2 m)

Description: A large-scaled, deep-bodied olive fish with mouth barbels (whiskers) and a forked, orangish tail.

Habitat: Found in clear and turbid streams, ponds and sloughs. Prefers warm water.

Comments: Introduced species is widely distributed throughout the U.S.

GIZZARD SHAD
Dorosoma cepedianum
Size: To 16 in. (40 cm)

Description: Blue to gray fish has silvery sides and a small mouth. The last dorsal fin ray is elongate and filamentous.

Habitat: Large rivers, lakes, reservoirs and estuaries with muddy bottoms.

Comments: Named for its gizzard organ – a sack filled with rocks – that aids in breaking down foods. Also called skipjack for its habit of skipping along the water's surface. Often occurs in large schools.

CHAIN PICKEREL
Esox niger
Size: To 30 in. (75 cm)

Description: Olive-to-brown fish has an elongate snout and sides marked with a dark, chain-like pattern. Undersides are whitish.

Habitat: Streams, rivers and lakes with abundant vegetation.

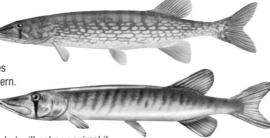

Comments: Feeds primarily on fish but will eat any animal it can swallow. Jaw is full of sharp, recurved teeth. The similar redfin pickerel (*E. americanus americanus*) has red-orange fins.

Redfin Pickerel

BROWN TROUT
Salmo trutta
Size: To 40 in. (1 m)

Description: Olive to brown above, it is covered with red, black or orange spots, often with white halos. Caudal fin is straight-edged. Interior of mouth is all white.

Habitat: Cool, fast-flowing streams and lakes. Some sea-run populations occur in nearshore waters.

Comments: An introduced species renowned for its wariness, it is prized by anglers.

RAINBOW TROUT
Oncorhynchus mykiss
Size: To 2 ft. (60 cm)

Description: A dark-spotted fish named for the distinctive reddish band running down its side. Band is most prominent during spring spawning. Rainbow trout that go to sea are called steelhead.

Habitat: Abundant in cold streams, reservoirs and lakes.

Comments: A popular food fish, it is one of the most common farmed fish. Weighs up to 42 lbs. (22 kg).

Steelhead

WHITE CRAPPIE
Pomoxis annularis
Size: To 20 in. (50 cm)

Description: Has a humped back,
6 dorsal spines, 6–9 dark side blotches
and a white belly.

Habitat: Sandy or muddy bottomed streams
and ponds, often in turbid water.

Comments: Is more tolerant of turbid water
than the black crappie. Weighs up to 5.3 lbs.
(2.4 kg).

BLACK CRAPPIE
Pomoxis nigromaculatus
Size: To 20 in. (50 cm)

Description: Mottled fish has dorsal fin set
well back on its hunched back. First of two
dorsal fins has 7–8 stiff spines.

Habitat: Quiet, clear lakes, ponds and rivers.

Comments: Also tolerant of silty water, it
is caught in a wide range of habitats. Can
see well in the dark and is most active
feeding in the evening. Often schools
around vertical structures.

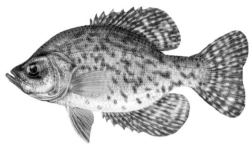

REDBREAST SUNFISH
Lepomis auritus
Size: To 11 in. (28 cm)

Description: Olive to bluish fish has a
yellow-orange belly, long, thin, black ear
flap and bluish lines on its cheek.

Habitat: Streams with sandy or gravelly
bottoms, ponds, lakes.

Comments: Typically a loner, it is more
common in streams than other sunfish.

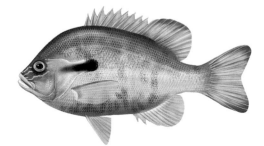

BLUEGILL
Lepomis macrochirus
Size: To 16 in. (40 cm)

Description: Flattened, dark olive fish has
brassy reflections. Ear flap is black. Note
dark spot at the rear of the soft dorsal fin.
Dusky side bars are often present.

Habitat: Quiet, well-vegetated streams,
lakes, ponds and rivers.

Comments: One of the most popular sport
fishes in the country, it is often stocked in
lakes and impoundments.

WARMOUTH
Lepomis gulosus
Size: To 12 in. (30 cm)

Description: Dark olive-brown, thick fish has mottled sides. Note dark lines radiating back from red eye. Belly is yellowish. Anal fin has 3 spines.

Habitat: Quiet water in well-vegetated streams, ponds, swamps and lakes.

Comments: Spends much of its time in dense vegetation feeding on aquatic insects, crayfish and small fishes.

GREEN SUNFISH
Lepomis cyanellus
Size: To 12 in. (30 cm)

Description: Robust, greenish, yellow-to-white bellied sunfish has a large mouth and dark spot on rear of second dorsal and anal fins. Upper jaw extends to beneath eye pupil.

Habitat: Clear ponds and streams with little current.

Comments: Tolerant of turbid water, it is very common and widespread in Texas. Weighs up to 4 lbs. (1.8 kg).

LONGEAR SUNFISH
Lepomis megalotis
Size: To 9 in. (23 cm)

Description: Olive to bluish fish has a yellow-orange belly and bluish lines on its face. Note long, white-edged black gill flap.

Habitat: Clear quiet waters with moderate vegetation.

Comments: Primarily a carnivore, it feeds on insects, snails and fishes. Weighs up to 1.7 lbs. (.8 kg).

REDEAR SUNFISH
Lepomis microlophus
Size: To 14 in. (35 cm)

Description: Olive to yellowish, it has a black gill flap edged in red and white. Female has an orange gill cover.

Habitat: Clear, quiet ponds, lakes and streams.

Comments: Also called shellcracker, it feeds on snails and clams that it crushes with molar-like teeth.

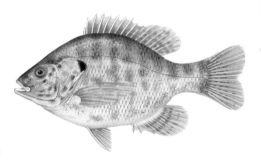

SPOTTED BASS
Micropterus punctulatus
Size: To 2 ft. (60 cm)
Description: Dark olive above, it has diamond-shaped mid-lateral blotches. Similar to the largemouth bass, its jaw line does not extend beyond the eye and has rows of small black spots below the lateral line.
Habitat: Warm rivers, ponds, lakes and reservoirs.
Comments: A prized sport fish that has been widely introduced.

GUADALUPE BASS
Micropterus treculii
Size: To 16 in. (40 cm)
Description: Greenish bass has 10–12 dark bars along its sides.
Habitat: Swift-moving streams and small to medium rivers.
Comments: Found only in Texas, it is endemic to the northern and eastern Edwards Plateau.

Texas' State Fish

SMALLMOUTH BASS
Micropterus dolomieu
Size: To 27 in. (68 cm)
Description: Brownish to greenish bass has vertical barring along its sides. Jaw margin does not extend beyond the eye. White belly does not extend high up sides.
Habitat: Cool streams, lakes, reservoirs.
Comments: Prefers cooler, deeper water than the largemouth bass.

LARGEMOUTH BASS
Micropterus salmoides
Size: To 38 in. (95 cm)
Description: Greenish, mottled fish with a dark, often blotched, side stripe. Has a large mouth with the upper jaw extending past the eye. White belly extends high up sides.
Habitat: Under protective cover in quiet, vegetated lakes, ponds, streams and rivers.
Comments: Weighs up to 22.3 lbs. (10 kg). The most sought-after game fish in Texas, there are hundreds of bass angling clubs in Texas devoted to fishing and conservation.

STRIPED BASS
Morone saxatilis
Size: To 6 ft. (1.8 m)
Description: Silvery-sided fish has 6–9 dark, uninterrupted side stripes.
Habitat: Coastal species moves far upstream in coastal rivers during spawning migrations.
Comments: Also called striper, rockfish and lineside, it has been widely introduced to freshwater habitats throughout Texas. The fourth most preferred species among licensed Texas anglers.

WHITE BASS
Morone chrysops
Size: To 18 in. (45 cm)
Description: Deep-bodied fish has silvery sides with 4–9 dark stripes, often interrupted below.
Habitat: Lakes, ponds, rivers.
Comments: Considered excellent fighters and prized table fare, they are the fifth most preferred species among licensed Texas anglers.

WIPER
Morone saxatilis x Morone chrysops
Size: To 20 in. (50 cm)
Description: Silvery fish has 6–9 broken side stripes.
Habitat: Ponds, rivers, lakes.
Comments: Hybrid between a striped bass and a white bass, it is a very popular, hard-fighting, sport fish and excellent table fish.

YELLOW BASS
Morone mississippiensis
Size: To 18 in. (45 cm)
Description: Silvery-yellow fish has 5–9 black stripes on sides. The lowermost stripes are broken posterior to the middle.
Habitat: Quiet streams, lakes, backwaters and rivers.
Comments: Lives in schools and feeds on insects, fishes and crustaceans. In spring it makes spawning runs up waterways.

AMERICAN EEL
Anguilla rostrata
Size: To 5 ft. (1.5 m)
Description: Typically dark green-brown in color, its body shape is distinctive.
Habitat: Anadromous.
Comments: Spends most of its life (up to 15 years) in freshwater before migrating to the Sargasso Sea to spawn and die. An exceptional food fish, in Texas it is usually caught by anglers who are fishing for something else.

SALTWATER FISHES

SPECKLED TROUT
Cynoscion nebulosus
Size: To 28 in. (70 cm)
Description: Blue-gray above and silvery-white below, it is black-spotted on its upper side, including dorsal and caudal fins.
Habitat: Estuaries, marshes, shallow coastal waters.
Comments: Also called spotted seatrout and spec, it is one of the most abundant coastal game fish and can be caught year-round. Weighs up to 17 lbs. (8 kg).

SOUTHERN FLOUNDER
Paralichthys lethostigma
Size: To 3 ft. (90 cm)
Description: Distinguished by its flat profile and long dorsal and anal fins.
Habitat: Over sandy and muddy bottoms to depths of 400 ft. (120 m).
Comments: The largest of 25 species of flatfishes found in Texas coastal waters. A prized food and game fish, it accounts for 95% of the flounder harvested in the state.

ATLANTIC STINGRAY
Dasyatis sabina
Size: To 2 ft. (60 cm) wide
Description: Small ray has a yellow-brown diamond-shaped disk and a triangular snout.
Habitat: Shallow estuaries or brackish habitats along the coastline.
Comments: Tail spine is venomous and can inflict painful wounds. Waders are encouraged to shuffle their feet when moving to frighten the rays away and avoid being stung.

ATLANTIC CROAKER
Micropogonias undulatus
Size: To 2 ft. (60 cm)

Description: Blue to grayish above, it has up to 20 oblique bars on its sides formed by brown dots on scales. Has a small terminal mouth and small barbels (whiskers) on its chin.

Habitat: Coastal bays and estuaries in summer, also ventures into freshwater.

Comments: Named for the noise it makes when the male vibrates its swim bladders during mating season.

GAFFTOPSAIL CATFISH
Bagre marinus
Size: To 40 in. (1 m)

Description: Bluish-silvery fish is named for its long dorsal fin that rises from its back like a sail. Note adipose fin and prominent chin barbels.

Habitat: Nearshore waters, estuaries.

Comments: Spines on dorsal and pectoral fins are covered in toxic slime and can inflict painful injuries.

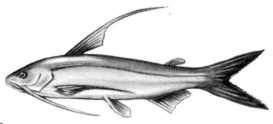

PINFISH
Lagodon rhomboides
Size: To 16 in. (40 cm)

Description: Bluish-brassy fish has a number of pale yellowish side stripes and a dark shoulder spot.

Habitat: Shallow, nearshore waters, often near piers.

Comments: Very common in coastal areas where shellfish are abundant.

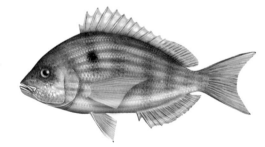

SHEEPSHEAD
Archosargus probatocephalus
Size: To 3 ft. (90 cm)

Description: Easily distinguished by its vivid black and white bars. Has large sharp spines on its dorsal fin.

Habitat: Shallow water over muddy bottoms, grassy areas.

Comments: Also called convict fish, it has strong teeth and grazes on hard-shelled barnacles and shellfish.

LANE SNAPPER
Lutjanus synagris
Size: To 14 in. (35 cm)
Description: Rosy-red to olivaceous fish has a large rounded dark spot beneath the soft dorsal fin. Has 8–10 yellow to gold stripes on body.
Habitat: Shallow coastal waters.
Comments: Also called candy snapper and spot snapper, it is often found in large schools.

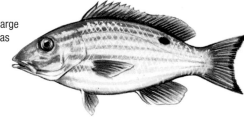

RED SNAPPER
Lutjanus campechanus
Size: To 3 ft. (90 cm)
Description: Scarlet above and rosy below. Note red iris and sharply pointed anal fin.
Habitat: Over rocks and reefs to depths of 300 ft. (100 m).
Comments: Considered the most sought-after offshore fish by commercial and sport anglers in Texas, it weighs up to 50 lbs. (23 kg).

BLACK DRUM
Pogonias cromis
Size: To 6 ft. (1.8 m)
Description: Deep-bodied, high-backed gray-to-bronze fish with black fins and 4–5 broad, dark side bars. Note long barbels under the lower jaw.
Habitat: Clear and muddy waters in surf zones, open ocean to depths of 100 ft. (30 m).
Comments: Has prominent teeth that it uses to crush the shells of mollusks and crustaceans. Often feeds in schools. A superior table fish, it is often featured in coastal restaurants.

REDFISH
Sciaenops ocellatus
Size: To 5 ft. (1.5 m)
Description: Reddish to copper colored fish has a dark spot at base of tail fin.
Habitat: Ranges from tidal lakes and grass flats through to the Gulf and along the Texas coast.
Comments: A very popular sport fish that will hit on most types of bait. Prized by surf-casters and waders. Also known as red drum, channel bass or simply reds, it weighs up to 94 lbs. (46 kg). The current Texas record is 59.5 lbs. (27 kg).

Texas' State Saltwater Fish

STRIPED MULLET
Mugil cephalus
Size: 9–19.5 in. (35–50 cm)

Description: Rounded fish has a blue-green back, a silvery body and dark longitudinal stripes along sides. Mouth is small.

Habitat: Coastal waters and estuaries, often ventures far inland into freshwater.

Comments: Often seen in nearshore waters jumping to evade predators, it is very common and one of the most important prey foods for other coastal fishes.

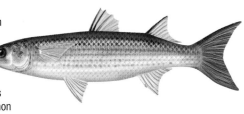

FLORIDA POMPANO
Trachinotus carolinus
Size: To 25 in. (63 cm)

Description: Deep-bodied fish is blue-green above with silvery sides. Belly is often yellowish. Blunt snout overhangs small mouth.

Habitat: Shallow nearshore waters.

Comments: Popular food and sport fish, it is a fast swimmer known for its leaping ability. Often caught by surf-casters, many consider it to be the most delicious Gulf fish.

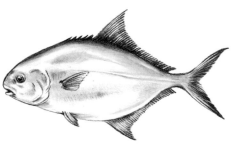

CREVALLE JACK
Caranx hippos
Size: To 40 in. (1 m)

Description: Deep-bodied greenish-blue fish has a yellowish belly. Note dark spot on gill cover and pectoral fin. Head has a steep profile.

Habitat: Nearshore and offshore waters.

Comments: Also known as jackfish, the Texas record fish weighed over 50 lbs. (23 kg).

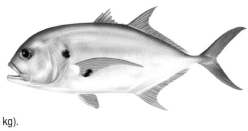

GREATER AMBERJACK
Seriola dumerili
Size: To 6 ft. (1.8 m)

Description: Brownish above, it has a diffuse yellow stripe along its midline. Note dark stripe from snout through eye toward dorsal fin.

Habitat: Coastal waters and open seas to depths of 1,200 ft. (360 m).

Comments: An important commercial and sport fish, the Texas record weighed 115 lbs. (52 kg).

SNOOK
Centropomus undecimalis
Size: To 4.5 ft. (1.4 m)

Description: Elongate, slender fish is green-brown above and whitish below. Key field marks are its concave, pointed snout, jutting lower jaw and dark side stripe.

Habitat: Fresh- and saltwater coastal areas, rivers.

Comments: A sleek, fast fish, it is a strong fighter popular with anglers. Feeds primarily on crustaceans and fish and is an esteemed table fish.

TARPON
Megalops atlanticus
Size: To 8 ft. (2.4 m)

Description: Huge, silvery, large-headed fish has a jutting lower jaw and a large mouth. Short dorsal fin has a thread-like trailing edge. Large, silvery scales are up to 3 in. (8 cm) in diameter.

Habitat: Shallow coastal waters.

Comments: Considered the "silverking" of sportfish, it is a powerful swimmer that makes spectacular leaps after being hooked. Weighs up to 286 lbs. (130 kg).

TRIPLETAIL
Lobotes surinamensis
Size: To 40 in. (1 m)

Description: Tan to dark brown, deep-bodied fish has elongate dorsal and anal fins that give it a 'triple-tailed' appearance.

Habitat: Nearshore waters, estuaries.

Comments: Often seen floating at the surface on its side, it is often mistaken for a dead leaf or floating debris. A good food fish.

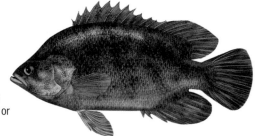

COBIA
Rachycentron canadum
Size: To 7 ft. (2.1 m)

Description: Long, dark brown fish with a flattened head has a dark side stripe. Low first dorsal fin has 7-9 spines. Caudal fin is deeply forked.

Habitat: Coastal and offshore waters, often around reefs and barrier islands.

Comments: A popular game and food fish that will take almost any bait. Weighs up to 135 lbs. (61 kg). Also called lemonfish, ling, black salmon, black kingfish, crab eater and runner.

DOLPHINFISH
Coryphaena hippurus
Size: To 7 ft. (2.1 m)

Description: Unmistakable snub-nosed fish is iridescent blue or green and has yellow sides flecked with spots. Note steep forehead and long dorsal and anal fins.

Habitat: Deep water offshore.

Comments: Also known as mahi-mahi and dorado. Once landed, its iridescent colors fade quickly. A popular sport and food fish, it weighs up to 87 lbs. (40 kg).

KING MACKEREL
Scomberomorus cavalla
Size: To 5 ft. (1.5 m)

Description: Dark bluish above and silvery below. First dorsal fin is silvery. Note sharp drop in lateral line under second dorsal fin.

Habitat: Coastal waters, offshore reefs.

Comments: The target of many fishing tournaments, it is an esteemed sport and food fish. Also known as kingfish, it weighs up to 93 lbs. (42 kg).

SAILFISH
Istiophorus platypterus
Size: To 11 ft. (3.3 m)

Description: Told by its huge, fan-shaped, retractable dorsal fin. Has a long, pointed, rigid snout that forms a bill or spear.

Habitat: Warm oceanic waters.

Comments: A predator, it uses its bill to slash or stab fish. Weighs up to 220 lbs. (100 kg).

BLUE MARLIN
Makaira nigricans
Size: To 14 ft. (4.2 m)

Description: Dark blue above and lighter below, it has a rigid dorsal fin and about 15 bars on its sides. Note steep head profile. Has long and pointed rigid bill.

Habitat: At surface to middle depths in open oceans.

Comments: A renowned fighting fish, it weighs up to 1,400 lbs. (636 kg). Both blue marlin and sailfish roam the deep waters closest to Port Isabela and the lower Texas coast and may move north as the summer progresses.

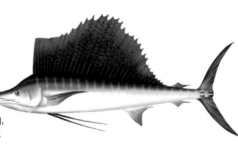

Butterflies and moths belong to the second largest order of insects (next to beetles) with approximately 170,000 species worldwide. All have two pairs of wings covered with overlapping layers of fine scales. They feed by uncoiling a long feeding-tube (proboscis) and sucking nutrients from flowers, puddles, etc. When not in use, the tube is coiled under the head.

The two groups differ in several ways:

BUTTERFLIES

- Active by day
- Brightly colored
- Thin body
- Rests with wings held erect over its back
- Antennae are thin and thickened at the tip

MOTHS

- Active at night
- Most are dull colored
- Stout body
- Rests with wings folded, tent-like, over its back
- Antennae are usually thicker and often feathery

All butterflies and moths have a complex life cycle consisting of four developmental stages.

1. **Eggs** – Eggs are laid singly or in clusters on vegetation or on the ground. One or more clutches of eggs may be laid each year.
2. **Caterpillars (larvae)** – These worm-like creatures hatch from eggs and feed primarily on plants (often on the host plant on which the eggs were laid). As they grow, larvae shed their skin periodically.
3. **Pupae** – Pupae are the 'cases' within which caterpillars transform into adults. The pupa of a butterfly is known as a chrysalis; those of moths are called cocoons. In cooler regions, pupae often over-winter before maturing into butterflies or moths.
4. **Adult** – Butterflies/moths emerge from pupae to feed and breed.

ATTRACTING BUTTERFLIES TO YOUR YARD

Food – Almost all butterfly caterpillars eat plants; adult butterflies feed almost exclusively on plant nectar. Your library or local garden shop will have information on which plants attract specific species.

Water – Soak the soil in your garden or sandy areas to create puddles. These provide a source of water and minerals.

Rocks – Put large flat rocks in sunny areas. Butterflies will gather there to spread their wings and warm up.

Brush – Small brush piles and hollow logs provide ideal places for butterflies to lay their eggs and hibernate over the winter.

SWALLOWTAILS & ALLIES

Family includes the largest butterfly species. Most are colorful and have a tail-like projection on each hindwing. All measurements denote wingspan.

PIPEVINE SWALLOWTAIL

Battus philenor – To 5 in. (13 cm)
Wings are dark black above with blue-green iridescence. Note white crescent-shaped marks on outer edge of hindwings.

EASTERN TIGER SWALLOWTAIL

Papilio glaucus – To 6 in. (15 cm)
Large black and yellow butterfly has yellow spots on its wing margins and a black tail on its hindwing.

BLACK SWALLOWTAIL

Papilio polyxenes – To 3.5 in. (9 cm)
Black to blue-black butterfly is yellow spotted and has bluish markings and orange eyespots near the rear of the hindwing.

GIANT SWALLOWTAIL

Papilio cresphontes – To 6 in. (15 cm)
Dark brownish forewings have a diagonal band of yellow spots. Tails have yellow centers edged in black.

PALAMEDES SWALLOWTAIL

Papilio palamedes – To 5 In. (13 cm)
Black-brown butterfly has wings with postmedian yellow bands. Hindwings have a marginal band of yellowish crescents.

SPICEBUSH SWALLOWTAIL

Papilio troilus – To 4.5 in. (11 cm)
Black forewings have ivory spots along the margin. Underwings are bluish-green on their outer half.

WHITES & SULPHURS

White and yellow/orange butterflies are among the first to appear in spring.

ORANGE SULPHUR

Colias eurytheme – To 2.5 in. (6 cm)
Bright gold-orange butterfly has dark to pinkish wing margins and prominent forewing spots.

SLEEPY ORANGE

Eurema nicippe – To 2 in. (5 cm)
Bright orange butterfly has wide black borders on wings and a small, dark forewing spot.

CABBAGE WHITE

Pieris rapae – To 2 in. (5 cm)
Small, milk-white butterfly has four dark spots on its forewings and hindwings.

SOUTHERN DOGFACE

Zerene cesonia – To 3 in. (8 cm)
Yellow and black butterfly has a poodle-head pattern on its forewings. A fast flier, it may be extremely prolific March–November in Texas.

SKIPPERS

Named for their fast, bouncing flight, skippers have distinctive antennae that end in curved clubs.

Underwings

SACHEM

Atalopedes campestris – To 1.5 in. (4 cm)
Tawny brown butterfly has a large black forewing patch. Found in pastures, fields, lawns, gardens and disturbed sites.

SILVER-SPOTTED SKIPPER

Epargyreus clarus – To 2.5 in. (6 cm)
Medium-sized brown butterfly has a large, irregular silver patch on the underside of its hindwings and yellowish spots across the middle of the forewing.

GOSSAMER-WINGED BUTTERFLIES

Family of small butterflies that often have small, hair-like tails on their hindwings. Many rest with their wings folded and underwings exposed.

TAILED BLUE

***Cupido* spp.** – To 1.25 in. (3.2 cm)
Bright lavender blue wings have white margins. Note orange spots near tail on hindwing (often absent). Found in meadows, canyons, fields and forest margins.

SPRING AZURE

Celastrina ladon – To 1.25 in. (3.2 cm)
Bright pale blue butterfly is widespread and common in woodlands, roadsides and brushy areas at all elevations.

Underwings

GRAY HAIRSTREAK

Strymon melinus – To 1.25 in. (3.2 cm)
Dark grayish underwings have bold orange and blue patches above tail. Upperwings are blue-gray.

GREAT PURPLE HAIRSTREAK

Atlides halesus – To 2 in. (5 cm)
Iridescent blue butterfly has two tails on each hindwing. Abdomen is blue above, red-orange below.

BRUSHFOOT BUTTERFLIES

Named for their small hairy forelegs which they use to 'taste' food.

MOURNING CLOAK

Nymphalis antiopa – To 3.5 in. (9 cm)
Rich brown-maroon wings are bordered by a cream-yellow band and blue submarginal spots.

COMMON WOOD NYMPH

Cercyonis pegala – To 3 in. (8 cm)
Large brown butterfly has 2 eyespots on the forewing and 1–2 on the hindwing.

MONARCH

Danaus plexippus – To 4 in. (10 cm)
Large cinnamon-orange butterfly has dark veins and rows of white spots on black wing margins. Found in meadows, fields and other open habitats.

VICEROY

Limenitis archippus – To 3 in. (8 cm)
Similar to the monarch but smaller, it has a thin black band on its hindwings. Believed to mimic the monarch because it is noxious to predators.

RED-SPOTTED PURPLE

Limenitis arthemis astyanax – To 4 in. (10 cm)
Blue to blue-green butterfly has iridescence on the outer part of the hindwing. Note red spots on forewing tips. Found in open woodlands, meadows and along waterways, shorelines and roads.

QUESTION MARK

Polygonia interrogationis – To 2.5 in. (6 cm)
Rust-orange butterfly has black blotches on wings. Ragged wing margins have lilac band. Silvery mark on hindwing resembles a question mark.

TEXAN CRESCENT

Anthanassa texana – To 2 in. (5 cm)
Mostly black with white dots and bars, its forewing is indented below the tip. Note white midband on hindwings. Found in open areas including deserts, scrublands, streamsides, parks and grasslands.

AMERICAN LADY

Vanessa virginiensis – To 2.5 in. (6 cm)
Unevenly-marked brown-yellow-orange butterfly has white bars and spots on the forewings and a row of black-trimmed blue spots on the outer hindwing. Also called hunter's butterfly and Virginia Lady.

BORDERED PATCH

Chlosyne lacinia – To 2 in. (5 cm)
Black butterfly has white or orange marginal
dots and wide orange patches on hindwings.
Found in oak woodlands, thorn forests,
deserts, fields and roadsides.

AMERICAN SNOUT

Libytheana carinenta – To 2 in. (5 cm)
Brown above with orange bands and white spots,
it is told at a glance by its squared off forewings
and projecting 'snout' (formed from projecting
mouth parts) that enclose its coiled proboscis.
Found in the vicinity of hackberries, the prime
larval host plant.

TAWNY EMPEROR

Asterocampa clyton – To 2.5 in. (6 cm)
Tawny orange-brown butterfly has yellow
spots on forewings and a row of black spots
along hindwings. Found in open deciduous
woodlands and along waterways and in cities
and parks containing hackberry trees.

QUEEN

Danaus gilippus – To 3.5 in. (9 cm)
Rich, chestnut brown-orange wings have black
margins and are finely spotted with white dots.
Found in open areas including deserts, fields,
roadways, pastures, dunes and along roadways
containing milkweeds.

HACKBERRY EMPEROR

Asterocampa celtis – To 2.5 in. (6 cm)
Brown to gray-brown butterfly has dark
forewing tips with white spots and a single
black eyespot lacking a pupil. Hackberry trees
are the only host plant for this species.

BUCKEYE

Junonia coenia – To 2.5 in. (6 cm)
Tawny to dark brown butterfly has wings
with scalloped edges. Note orange forewing
bars and eight distinct eyespots. The
eyespots are believed to scare off predators.

RED ADMIRAL

Vanessa atalanta – To 2.5 in. (6 cm)
Dark butterfly has prominent orange-red to
vermillion bars on forewings and on hindwing
border. Note white spots at apex of forewings.
Also called alderman.

VARIEGATED FRITILLARY

Euptoieta claudia – To 3 in. (8 cm)
Tawny orange butterfly has upperwings with
thick, dark veins and black spots near margins.
Note zigzag band in the middle of both wings.

JULIA

Dryas iulia – To 3.5 in. (9 cm)
Bright orange butterfly has long, narrow wings
with a narrow black border on the hindwing.
Found in subtropical hammocks, islands,
gardens and fields.

ZEBRA LONGWING

Heliconius charithonia – To 4 in. (10 cm)
Long, narrow wings have yellow bands and a row
of yellow spots at the base of the hindwing. Found
in wet habitats including tropical hammocks,
moist forests and fields.

MOTHS

BLACK WITCH

Ascalapha odorata – To 6 in. (15 cm)
Large brown-black moth has pointed
forewings and a series of undulating light and
dark lines on both wings. Found in subtropical
forests with pea plants. In south Texas, legend
has it that if a black witch moth lands above
your door and stays there for a while you will
win the lottery. In Central American cultures, it
is associated with death and misfortune.

CECROPIA MOTH

Hyalophora cecropia – To 7 in. (18 cm)
North America's largest native moth has dark
brown-rusty wings with white, hair-like scales
that gives them a frosted appearance. Note
prominent crescent spots and red-banding on
wings. Body is red with white banding.

IMPERIAL MOTH

Eacles imperialis – To 7 in. (18 cm)
Yellow wings have pinkish-brown
to purplish-brown marks and brown
speckles. Host plants include pines,
maples, oaks, spruce and sweetgum.

POLYPHEMUS MOTH

Antheraea polyphemus – To 6 in. (15 cm)
Large, tan-colored moth has two yellow
forewing eyespots and two yellow hindwing
eyespots surrounded by blue and black.
Males have bushy antennae.

AMERICAN TENT
CATERPILLAR MOTH

Malacosoma americanum –
To 1.5 in. (4 cm)
Stout, furry moth has brown to gray
forewings crossed by two light bands.
Caterpillar is orange-brown with blue
dots on its sides and back. When the
larvae hatch in spring, they weave silken
'tents' between the branches of trees.
Considered pests, the caterpillars often
defoliate and kill the host tree.

Tent Caterpillar
Web

LUNA MOTH

Actias luna – To 7 in. (18 cm)
One of the largest moths in North America, it has
lime green wings and a white body. Note long,
sweeping tail on hindwings. Found primarily in
deciduous forests.

WHITE-LINED SPHINX

Hyles lineata – To 3.5 in. (9 cm)
Stout, furry moth has white stripes on the
forewings and a thick pink stripe on the
hindwings. Caterpillar has a red 'horn' at
its rear. Active at all hours, it hovers like a
hummingbird near flowers.

♀

IO MOTH

Automeris io – To 3 in. (8 cm)
Male forewings are yellowish, females are
red-brown. Hindwings have prominent
eyespots ringed with black-blue and yellow.
Female is brownish. Male is yellowish.
Caterpillar spines can cause painful stings.

TREES

Trees can be broadly defined as perennial woody plants at least 16 ft. (5 m) tall with a single stem and a well-developed crown of branches, twigs and leaves. Most are long-lived plants and range in age from 40–50 years for smaller deciduous trees to several hundred years for many of the conifers.

A tree's size and shape is largely determined by its genetic makeup, but growth is also affected by environmental factors such as moisture, light and competition from other species. Trees growing in crowded stands will often only support compact crowns due to the competition for light. Some species at high altitudes grow gnarled and twisted as a result of exposure to high winds.

Common Tree Silhouettes

| Pine | Juniper | Willow | Oak | Cottonwood |

SHRUBS

Shrubs are perennial woody plants normally less than 16 ft. (5 m) tall that support a crown of branches, twigs and leaves. Unlike trees, they are anchored to the ground by several stems rather than a single trunk. Most are fast-growing and provide an important source of food and shelter for wildlife.

N.B. – Some shrubs that are most conspicuous when in bloom are included in the following section on flowering plants.

How to Identify Trees and Shrubs

First, note its size and shape. Does it have one or several 'trunks?' Examine the size, color, and shape of the leaves and how they are arranged on the twigs. Are they opposite or alternate? Simple or compound? Hairy or smooth? Are flowers or fruits visible on branches or on the ground? Once you've collected as much information as you can, consult the illustrations and text to confirm your sighting.

SIMPLE LEAF SHAPES

| Elliptical | Heart-shaped | Rounded | Oval | Lobed | Lance-shaped |

COMPOUND LEAVES

Leaflets

LEAF ARRANGEMENTS

Alternate   Opposite   Whorled

COMMON FRUITS

Drupe
junipers, cherries,
dogwoods, hollies

Pome
apples, plums,
yuccas, pears

Nut
walnuts, pecans,
hickories

Berry
blackberries,
raspberries

Winged Seed
dandelions,
milkweeds,
poplars,
cottonwoods

Samara
maples, ashes,
hophornbeams,
elms

Acorn
oaks

Pod
peas,
mesquites,
locusts

PINES

Most have long, needle-like leaves that grow grouped in bundles of 2–5. Male and female cones usually occur on the same tree.

SHORTLEAF PINE
Pinus echinata
Size: To 100 ft. (30 m)
Description: Tall, slender tree. Needles occur in bundles of 2 and are up to 5 in. (13 cm) long. Egg-shaped cones occur in clusters and are up to 2.5 in. (6 cm) long.
Habitat: Well drained uplands in east Texas.
Comments: An important timber species, its lumber is used in construction, millwork and for the production of barrels.

LONGLEAF PINE
Pinus palustris
Size: To 130 ft. (40 m)
Description: Straight-trunked tree has very long needles (to 18 in./45 cm) arranged into tight bundles of 3. The needles grow in rounded clusters at the ends of branches, giving the tree a tufted appearance. Cylindrical cones are up to 12 in. (30 cm) long and have thin prickles at the scale tips.
Habitat: Poor soils on prairies and scrub lands in east Texas.
Comments: A valuable source of food and cover for wildlife.

LOBLOLLY PINE
Pinus taeda
Size: To 125 ft. (38 m)
Description: Large fast-growing tree has a dense, rounded crown. Needles grow in bundles of 3 and are up to 10 in. (25 cm) long. Woody cones are stalkless and have prickles at the tips of the scales.
Habitat: Ranges from flood plains to hilly uplands in east Texas.
Comments: Fast-growing species is extensively cultivated for lumber and pulpwood. One definition of the word "loblolly" is mud puddle, a place where this species often grows.

CYPRESSES & ALLIES

All have scaly or awl-shaped leaves that are tightly bunched together on twigs. The heavily-weighted twigs usually droop at their tips and give the plants a relaxed profile.

JUNIPER
Juniperus spp.

Size: To 50 ft. (15 m)

Description: Shrub or small tree is distinguished by its scale-like or awl-like leaves that grow closely along twigs, often overlapping. Fruit is a berry-like cone.

Habitat: Dry, rocky soils.

Comments: Three species are found in Texas. Fruit is a favorite of birds, which disperse the seeds.

BALDCYPRESS FAMILY

Large trees have thick, buttressed trunks and live up to 1,000 years.

BALDCYPRESS
Taxodium distichum

Size: To 130 ft. (40 m)

Description: Distinguished by its flaring trunk and long, feathery leaves. In water, protruding root "knees" may be visible. Small rounded cones often hang in pairs.

Habitat: Swamps and along waterways in south-central and eastern Texas.

Comments: Branches are often draped with the common southern air plant, Spanish moss. The wood is prized because it resists decay.

WILLOWS & ALLIES

Most have narrow, finely-toothed leaves that grow alternately along twigs. Flowers often appear in spring before the leaves along semi-erect catkins.

BLACK WILLOW
Salix nigra

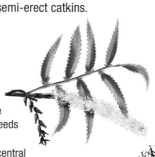

Size: To 50 ft. (15 m)

Description: Large tree may have one or more trunks. Slender, toothed, alternate leaves are up to 6 in. (15 cm) long. Fuzzy, elongate flower clusters are succeeded by a long string of capsules that contain seeds attached to long, silky hairs.

Habitat: Along streams and in wet areas throughout central and eastern Texas.

Comments: Bark contains salicylic acid (a component of aspirin) and extracts that were used by Native Americans to treat headaches.

SYCAMORES

Large trees with very stout trunks and distinctive 'buttonball' fruits.

AMERICAN SYCAMORE
Platanus occidentalis

Size: To 100 ft. (30 m)

Description: Large tree has an oval or round spreading crown. Alternate leaves are up to 12 in. (30 cm) wide and have broad, short-pointed lobes. Bark is gray-white and separated into thin scales that resemble pieces of a jigsaw puzzle. Fruit is a spiny ball that contains nutlets attached to long hairs.

Habitat: Found along waterways and in bottomlands and flood plains in eastern Texas.

Comments: Considered the largest deciduous tree in North America.

POPLARS

Found in moist habitats, these fast-growing trees are distinguished from willows by their drooping flower clusters (catkins).

EASTERN COTTONWOOD
Populus deltoides

Size: To 100 ft. (30 m)

Description: Large tree with an open crown of spreading branches. Large leaves up to 7 in. (18 cm) long have rounded teeth on edges. Flowers bloom in long clusters and are succeeded by capsules containing seeds attached to silky hairs.

Habitat: Moist soils in east and central Texas.

Comments: Often grows in association with willows. One of the fastest growing trees, it is often planted as a shade tree and in shelterbelts.

ELMS

Trees and shrubs all have short-stemmed, double-toothed leaves and distinctive, wafer-like fruits.

CEDAR ELM
Ulmus crassifolia

Size: To 80 ft. (24 m)

Description: Straight-trunked tree has a rounded crown of drooping branches. Alternate, elliptical leaves are up to 2.5 in. (6 cm) long. Short-stalked flowers are succeeded by distinctive wafer-like, samara (fruits) that are notched at the tip.

Habitat: Moist areas, upland limestone hills in eastern and central Texas.

Comments: The second most commonly planted native tree in Texas. Also referred to as "the poor man's live oak."

AMERICAN ELM
Ulmus americana

Size: To 100 ft. (30 m)

Description: Note vase-shaped profile. Alternate, toothed leaves are up to 6 in. (15 cm) long. Greenish flowers appear in spring before the leaves. Fruit is an oval samara. The seed is enclosed in a papery envelope with fuzzy edges that is notched at the tip.

Habitat: Moist, well-drained soils, mixed forests in eastern and central Texas.

Comments: Once the most commonly planted street tree in the early 20th Century, it was almost wiped out by Dutch elm disease that killed an estimated 77 million trees in the northern U.S. in the 1930s.

OAKS

Oaks represent a group of important hardwoods. Generally, they are large trees with stout trunks and spreading crowns that produce acorns for fruit.

LIVE OAK
Quercus virginiana

Size: To 60 ft. (18 m)

Description: Large, stately tree has a spreading crown and is often wider than it is tall. Stiff alternate leaves are leathery and have rolled edges. Dark acorns have a small cup that encloses about one quarter of the nut.

Habitat: Sandy soils, hammocks, rich woods along waterways in central and southeastern Texas.

Comments: Trees occurring along the coast are often shrubby. It is the most commonly planted native tree in Texas.

BLACKJACK OAK
Quercus marilandica

Size: To 60 ft. (18 m)

Description: Medium-sized, scrubby tree has a dense crown of stiff, drooping branches. Leathery leaves are broadest at the tip and have 3 lobes. Acorn has a thick brown cup. Bark is blackish.

Habitat: Dry and poorly drained soils in eastern and central Texas.

Comments: Named for its leaves that resemble the infamous lead-filled weapon. Heavy, hard wood is used for railroad ties, posts and is made into charcoal.

SHUMARD OAK
Quercus shumardii

Size: To 100 ft. (30 m)

Description: Large lowland tree has a rounded, open crown. Leaves have 5–9 lobes with bristly edges and are up to 8 in. (20 cm) long. Egg-shaped acorns have a shallow, saucer-like cup.

Habitat: Moist, well-drained soils in central and eastern Texas.

Comments: Leaves turn red or brown in autumn. Acorns are an important food source for deer, bears, raccoons, turkeys, squirrels and other rodents.

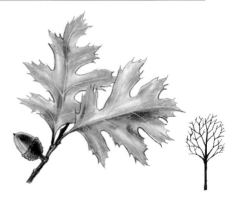

BUR OAK
Quercus macrocarpa

Size: To 80 ft. (24 m)

Description: Large tree has a stout trunk and a broad, rounded crown. Leaves are broadest above the middle, have 5–9 lobes and are up to 12 in. (30 cm) long. Large acorns have mossy, fringed cups and are up to 2 in. (5 cm) long.

Habitat: Limestone uplands, sandy plains and gravelly ridges in central Texas.

Comments: Acorns are the largest of any native oak. Planted for shade, ornament and shelterbelts.

POST OAK
Quercus stellata

Size: To 50 ft. (15 m)

Description: Tree has a short trunk and a compact, rounded crown. Distinctive leaves resemble a Maltese cross and have 5–7 deep lobes. Bowl-shaped acorns are up to .8 in. (2 cm) long.

Habitat: Rocky and sandy ridges, dry woodlands in central and eastern Texas.

Comments: Slow-growing tree is drought-resistant and doesn't reach flowering age for 20–30 years. It is so common it influenced the naming of a region – the Post Oak Savanna.

PEAS & ALLIES

Most members of this large family of trees, shrubs and herbs produce fruit in seed pods.

HONEY MESQUITE
Prosopis glandulosa

Size: To 40 ft. (12 m)

Description: Shrub or small tree with crown of crooked, thorny branches. Leaves are up to 10 in. (25 cm) long and have 7 to 20 pairs of leaflets. Distinctive fruit is a narrow pod that holds up to 20 seeds.

Habitat: Grasslands, sandy soils, deserts statewide except for east Texas.

Comments: Wood is an excellent source of firewood, charcoal and fence posts. Named for its seeds encased in a thick, sweet pulp that Native Americans used in foods and drinks.

EASTERN REDBUD
Cercis canadensis

Size: To 40 ft. (12 m)

Description: Short-trunked tree has an open crown of spreading branches. Showy, pea-shaped, pinkish to lavender flowers bloom in long clusters in spring and are succeeded by long seed pods in summer

Habitat: Moist soils, river bottoms, hardwood forests in east and central Texas.

Comments: Often planted as an ornamental, it is one of the first trees to bloom in the spring. Flowers are edible and often eaten in salads or fried.

CATCLAW ACACIA
Acacia greggii

Size: To 23 ft. (7 m)

Description: Gray-green deciduous shrub has short, curved spines along its branches. Leaves have 2–3 side branches, each with 4–6 pairs of leaflets. Fuzzy yellow flowers bloom in elongated spikes between April–October and are succeeded by twisted reddish seed pods.

Habitat: Rocky slopes, desert flats in west and central Texas.

Comments: A notorious local plant, its strong, curved spines readily tear clothing and flesh. Often forms impenetrable thickets.

MISCELLANEOUS FAMILIES

Following are common and distinctive Texas trees that belong to a diverse array of families.

TEXAS PERSIMMON
Diospyros texana

Size: To 40 ft. (12 m)

Description: Small tree with an open, oval crown. Simple, alternate, leathery leaves are short-stemmed. Flowers are succeeded by a sweet, round, edible fruit that is slightly depressed at the tip.

Habitat: Dry and rocky areas in central, western and southern Texas.

Comments: Native species is also known as capote and black persimmon. Wood is heavy and black and resembles ebony. The bark of mature trees peels away to reveal shades of gray, white and pink on the trunk underneath.

TEXAS ASH
Fraxinus texensis

Size: To 40 ft. (12 m)

Description: Medium-sized tree with a short trunk and large oval crown. Large, opposite compound leaves have rounded leaflets up to 3 in. (8 cm) long. Purplish flowers bloom in small clusters and are succeeded by long papery samaras, each containing a single seed.

Habitat: Rocky slopes, canyons, open forests in central and southern Texas.

Comments: Native species. Wood is strong, heavy and hard and used in construction.

BLACK WALNUT
Juglans nigra

Size: To 100 ft. (30 m)

Description: Large tree with a straight trunk and an open, rounded crown. Alternate, compound leaves have 15–23 leaflets and are up to 2 ft. (60 cm) long. Flowers are succeeded by large, round, leathery nuts to 2.5 in. (6 cm) in diameter.

Habitat: Bottomlands, floodplains and moist hillsides in east Texas.

Comments: Wood is coveted for furniture, gunstocks and veneer. Oily nuts are an important food source for squirrels and other wildlife.

TEXAS MADRONE
Arbutus texana

Size: To 30 ft. (9 m)

Description: Small tree often has multiple, twisted trunks. Leathery, evergreen alternate leaves are up to 5 in. (13 cm) long. Small clusters of bell-shaped flowers are succeeded by bright red-orange berries. Bark is bone white beneath. As the plant ages, the outer bark peels away in strips exposing the lighter bark beneath.

Habitat: Canyons and mountainsides in central and west Texas.

Comments: Heavy wood is used for tool handles, fuel and charcoal.

Bark

SWEETGUM
Liquidambar styraciflua

Size: To 120 ft. (36.5 m)

Description: Large tree has spreading conical crown. Star-shaped leaves have 5–7 lobes and are 6 in. (15 cm) long. Small, greenish flowers bloom in tight, round clusters and are succeeded by hard, round fruits covered with woody spines. The fruits often persist into winter.

Habitat: Floodplains, moist valleys, mixed woodlands in east Texas.

Comments: An important commercial species renowned for its tough, hard wood. The gummy, fragrant tree resin was once used to manufacture drugs and chewing gum.

PECAN
Carya illinoensis

Size: To 120 ft. (36.5 m)

Description: Large tree has a broad, spreading crown. Alternate, compound leaves are up to 20 in. (50 cm) long. Flowers bloom in long catkins and are succeeded by cylindrical oval nuts to 2 in. (5 cm) long.

Habitat: Fertile bottomlands in eastern and central Texas.

Comments: Native species is one of the most valuable cultivated crops in North America. Wood is used for furniture, flooring and smoking meat.

Texas' State Tree

SOUTHERN MAGNOLIA
Magnolia grandiflora

Size: To 100 ft. (30 m)

Description: Typically a large tree with a conical crown. Evergreen, glossy leaves are up to 10 in. (25 cm) long. Large creamy flowers to 8 in. (20 cm) in diameter have 9–14 petals. Cone-like, hairy fruits have bright red seeds.

Habitat: Rich woodlands, hammocks, along waterways.

Comments: Native to east Texas, it is widely planted throughout the state as an ornamental.

TEXAS SUGARBERRY
Celtis laevigata

Size: To 90 ft. (27 m)

Description: Large tree has a crown of light green foliage. Bark is very corky to warty in appearance. Alternate, long-pointed leaves are up to 5 in. (13 cm) long. Inconspicuous flowers are succeeded by orange-red berries that turn dark purple with age.

Habitat: Well-drained soils and riverbottoms in the eastern two thirds of the state.

Comments: Sweet fruits are an important food source for a variety of birds. Also called hackberry.

Bark

RED MAPLE
Acer rubrum

Size: To 90 ft. (27 m)

Description: Tree has a large crown of spreading branches. Leaves have 3–5 lobes and turn scarlet in autumn. Reddish flowers bloom in drooping clusters and are succeeded by red, winged seed pairs (double samara or "key").

Habitat: Moist soils in a variety of habitats in eastern Texas.

Comments: A fast-growing species often planted as a shade tree in urban areas.

OSAGE-ORANGE
Maclura pomifera

Size: To 40 ft. (12 m)

Description: Medium-sized tree has crown of crooked, interweaving thorny branches. Simple, alternate leaves have pointed tips and are up to 5 in. (13 cm) long. Flowers bloom in linear clusters and are succeeded by large, spherical green fruits to 5 in. (13 cm) in diameter.

Habitat: Moist soils in river valleys in eastern and southern Texas.

Comments: Native species is also known as bois d'arc, bodark and hedge apple. Bois d'arc is French for "bow wood" and Native Americans used the flexible wood for bows and war clubs.

RED MULBERRY
Morus rubra

Size: To 50 ft. (15 m)

Description: Simple alternate leaves are up to 9 in. (23 cm) long and may be heart- or mitten-shaped with 3–5 lobes. Cylindrical flower clusters are succeeded by a composite fruit that looks like an elongate blackberry. Fruits turn dark purple when mature.

Habitat: Moist soils in east and central Texas.

Comments: Edible fruits are an important food source for birds and wildlife. The Texas mulberry (*M. microphylla*) is found scattered throughout western Texas.

Texas Mulberry

BLACK CHERRY
Prunus serotina

Size: To 80 ft. (24 m)

Description: Large tree has aromatic bark and foliage that has a cherry-like odor. Simple, alternate leaves are up to 6 in. (15 cm) long. Drooping clusters of white flowers are succeeded by blackish cherries.

Habitat: Moist soils in a variety of habitats in east and south Texas.

Comments: Next to walnut, black cherry lumber has a greater value per board foot than any other hardwood. The wood is used primarily for furniture and paneling. The berries are used to make cough medicine, jelly and wine.

CRAPEMYRTLE
Lagerstroemia indica

Size: To 26 ft. (8 m)

Description: Multi-trunked tree or shrub has muscular limbs and a vase-shaped crown. Simple, alternate leaves are up to 3 in. (8 cm) long. Showy pink/red/purple/white flowers bloom in large spikes and have petals that resemble crepe paper.

Habitat: Drought resistant hardy plant thrives in most soils. Commonly found in north Texas.

Comments: Also called June Rose, Lilac of the South. Probably the most common landscape tree or shrub planted in Texas. Native to China.

Texas' State Shrub

BUSH PALMETTO
Sabal minor

Size: To 10 ft. (3 m)

Description: Medium-sized evergreen shrub or small tree. Huge fan-shaped leaves are distinctive with blades up to 5 ft. (1.5 m) long.

Habitat: Sandy and well-drained soils on the Texas coastal plain.

Comments: Also called dwarf palmetto, it often grows very close to the ground. The similar Texas palmetto (*S. texana*) is restricted to the lower Rio Grande Valley in extreme southern Texas.

TEXAS SAGE
Leucophyllum frutescens

Size: To 5 ft. (1.5 m)

Description: Grayish shrub has leaves covered with silvery hairs. Bright pink-lavender flowers are bell-shaped and up to 1 in. (3 cm) wide.

Habitat: Ditches, ravines, hillsides on well-drained soils.

Comments: Flowers are a favorite of butterflies. Widely planted as an ornamental throughout Texas.

Texas' State Native Shrub

YAUPON
Ilex vomitoria

Size: To 25 ft. (7.6 m)

Description: Thicket-forming, evergreen shrub or small tree. Shiny, alternate leaves have wavy teeth and are up to 2 in. (5 cm) long. Small white flowers are succeeded by shiny berry-like fruits clustered along twigs that persist into winter.

Habitat: Moist soils along coasts and in valleys in southeastern Texas.

Comments: Twigs and berries of this holly are a common Christmas ornamental. Europeans incorrectly assumed an infusion of this plant could induce vomiting. It is the only known North American plant that produces caffeine.

WILD AZALEA
Rhododendron canescens

Size: To 18 ft. (5.4 m)

Description: Showy, multi-trunked shrub has alternate leaves that are dark green above and silky to the touch. Sticky, pinkish, fragrant flowers bloom in whorl-like clusters. Five stamens extend far beyond the 5 petal-like lobes.

Habitat: Moist woodlands, swamp margins and along waterways.

Comments: The most common southeastern azalea, it tends to form large colonies. All parts of the plant are highly toxic. Also known as bush honeysuckle.

FLOWERING DOGWOOD
Cornus florida

Size: To 35 ft. (10.5 m)

Description: Small to medium-sized shrub or tree. Opposite, long-pointed leaves are up to 5 in. (13 cm) long. Tiny white to pinkish-white flowers have 4 white, pink or red, petal-like bracts and bloom in crowded clusters. Flowers are succeeded by shiny, red berry-like fruits.

Habitat: Moist and dry soils in valleys and uplands and in understory of hardwood forests in eastern Texas.

Comments: A popular ornamental, its showy flowers bloom early in the spring; the foliage is scarlet in autumn.

Wildflowers are soft-stemmed flowering plants, usually smaller than trees or shrubs, that grow anew each year. Some regenerate annually from the same rootstock (perennials), while others grow from seeds and last a single season (annuals). Most have flowering stems bearing colorful blossoms that ripen into fruits as the growing season progresses. The flowering stem typically grows upright, but may be climbing, creeping or trailing.

N.B. – This section covers wildflowers and includes some shrubs that are conspicuous when in bloom.

The species in this section have been grouped according to color rather than family to facilitate field identification. The color groups used are:

- White
- Yellow, Orange and Green
- Red and Pink
- Blue and Purple

How to Identify Wildflowers

After noting color, examine the shape of the flower heads. Are they daisy-like, bell-shaped, or cross-shaped? How are they arranged on the plant? Do they occur singly or in clusters? Are the flower heads upright or drooping? Pay close attention to the leaves and how they are arranged on the stem. Refer to the illustrations and text to confirm its size, habitat and blooming period.

N.B. – The blooming periods of flowers can vary depending on latitude, elevation and the weather. The seasons given are meant to serve as general guidelines only.

Remember that flowers are wildlife and should be treated as such. Many species have been seriously depleted due to loss of habitat and overpicking. In many areas, once-abundant species are now rare. Bring along a sketchbook and camera to record the flowers you see instead of picking them. This will help ensure there are more blossoms for you and others to enjoy in years to come.

N.B. – It is illegal to collect most of Texas' native plants. Check with the Department of Forestry regarding protected and endangered species.

FLOWER STRUCTURE

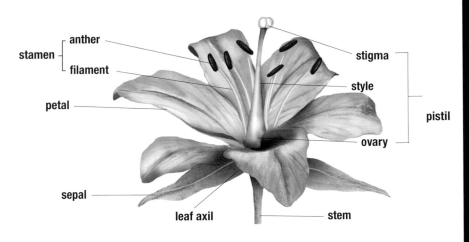

FLOWER SHAPES

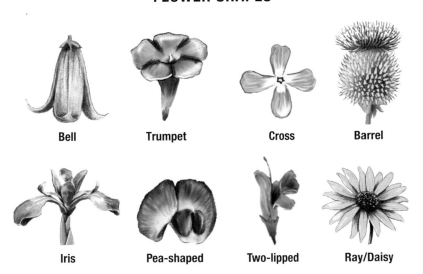

Bell	Trumpet	Cross	Barrel
Iris	Pea-shaped	Two-lipped	Ray/Daisy

WHITE FLOWERS

WHITE PRICKLY POPPY
Argemone albiflora

Size: To 3 ft. (90 cm)

Description: Tall, bristly stem supports a cupped, white flower with 4–6 petals.

Habitat: Gravelly and sandy soils in waste areas, roadsides, fields, pastures in central and eastern Texas.

Comments: Most plant parts are toxic if ingested. Blooms March–July. The closely related red prickly poppy (*A. sangunea*) is common in the South Texas Plains.

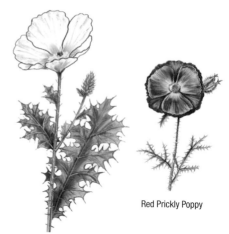

Red Prickly Poppy

MORNING GLORY
Ipomoea spp.

Size: Vine to 20 ft. (6 m)

Description: Family of vines and herbs has handsome funnel-shaped flowers. Flower color varies from white to pink/red and purple.

Habitat: Coastal dunes, fields, roadsides, disturbed areas.

Comments: An important coastal species, beach morning glory (*I. stolonifera*) helps to stabilize the dunes along the Gulf Coast. For many species in this family, the flowers bloom at night. Blooms April–December.

BLACKFOOT DAISY
Melampodium leucanthum

Size: To 12 in. (30 cm)

Description: Low, bushy plant has flowerheads with 8–13 broad white rays surrounding a central yellow disk.

Habitat: Gravelly and rocky soils.

Comments: One of the most drought-tolerant plants in Texas, it blooms March–November.

SPIDER LILY
Hymenocallis spp.

Size: To 3 ft. (90 cm)

Description: Strap-like leaves occur in a basal cluster. Two-edged stem supports 2–3 snow white flowers with "spidery" sepals to 7 in. (18 cm) across.

Habitat: Marshes, along streams and ditches.

Comments: Blooms May–August. All plant parts are toxic.

YUCCA
Yucca spp.

Size: 10–16 ft. (3–4.8 m)

Description: Tree or shrub with upright branches and prominent, dagger-like leaves. Creamy white, bell-shaped flowers bloom in a terminal cluster April–June. Flowers are succeeded by cylindrical fruits.

Habitat: Found on dry soils at elevations to 5,000 ft. (1,500 m).

Comments: Native Americans obtained food, soap, baskets and ropes from this plant.

WHITE DOGSTOOTH VIOLET
Erythronium albidum

Size: To 10 in. (25 cm)

Description: Thick, basal leaves are mottled, tapered at both ends and up to 8 in. (20 cm) long. Bare stems support a single, bell-shaped flower that is often tinged with lavender on the outside.

Habitat: Rich, moist soils along slopes and in understory of shady forests.

Comments: Often forms extensive colonies spreading from underground stems. Blooms February–May.

WHITE SNAKEROOT
Eupatorium rugosum

Size: To 3 ft. (90 cm)

Description: Firm stems support terminal clusters of white, fuzzy, rayless flowerheads. Ovate leaves are opposite and sharply toothed.

Habitat: Woods and thickets.

Comments: Blooms July–October and often forms large colonies. Supposedly capable of curing snakebite, all parts of the plant are poisonous and cattle that graze on it get the "trembles."

CRIMSON-EYED ROSE MALLOW
Hibiscus moscheutos

Size: To 8 ft. (2.4 m)

Description: Shrubby perennial has heart-shaped leaves that are gray-green above and white-hairy below. Showy, 5-petaled creamy white flowers are reddish at their base from which a tubular column of stamens extend.

Habitat: Tidal and freshwater marshes, wetlands.

Comments: Blooms July–September.

RAIN LILY
Cooperia drummondii

Size: To 12 in. (30 cm)

Description: Each stem supports a single, fragrant, flaring white flowerhead.

Habitat: Moist soils in grassy areas.

Comments: Blooms May–September, often appearing in large numbers after heavy rains. Two to four days after blooming the flowers turn pink and wither.

YELLOW, ORANGE & GREEN FLOWERS

INDIAN BLANKET
Gaillardia pulchella

Size: To 2 ft. (60 cm)

Description: Much-branched, hairy stems are leafy near the base. Fiery, pinwheel-shaped flowers have red rays often tipped in yellow. Inner disk is maroon and dome-shaped. Blooms throughout the year.

Habitat: Sandy soils, disturbed areas, roadsides, beaches, fields, pastures.

Comments: Conspicuous along roadsides, they often blanket large open areas. Also called firewheel.

BLACK-EYED SUSAN
Rudbeckia hirta

Size: To 3 ft. (90 cm)

Description: Flowers have 8–20 long yellow rays (often drooping) surrounding a brown, cone-shaped central disk. Stems and leaves are bristly to the touch.

Habitat: Waste areas, fields, prairies, open woodlands, roadsides.

Comments: Native Americans used it for fabric dye and tea. Extracts of the juice were used to relieve earaches.

PRICKLY PEAR CACTUS
Opuntia spp.

Size: To 7 ft. (2.1 m)

Description: Clump forming cactus has flat, fleshy green pads covered in sharp spines. Yellow flowers are succeeded by a fleshy, red, edible fruit ("tuna") covered in spines.

Habitat: Sandy and rocky areas on dry soil.

Comments: Both the pads and the fruit are edible. A simple way to remove the outer spines is to burn them off in a fire. The sweet fruits can be eaten raw or made into a jam or candy.

Texas' State Plant

CONEFLOWER
Ratibida columnifera

Size: To 4 ft. (1.2 m)

Description: Lacy foliage is divided into thread-like segments. Flowerheads have a long central disk (gray-green at first, turning brown as it matures) surrounded by drooping yellow rays.

Habitat: Dry prairies, pastures and woodlands.

Comments: Also called Mexican hat and prairie coneflower, it blooms February–October.

BUTTERFLYWEED
Asclepias tuberosa

Size: To 3 ft. (90 cm)

Description: Lance-shaped, alternate leaves are up to 5 in. (13 cm) long. Bright orange, star-like flowers bloom in large clusters May–September. Stem may be erect or crawling.

Habitat: Meadows, fields, roadsides, prairies, thickets.

Comments: Unlike other milkweed species, it lacks milky sap. As its name suggests, it is a favorite of butterflies, hummingbirds and other pollinators. The seeds and roots were once used as a mild laxative and to treat lung problems. The roots and plant sap are poisonous. Blooms April–September.

GOLDENROD
Solidago spp.

Size: To 8 ft. (2.4 m)

Description: Tall, leafy plant has long, arching cluster of tiny yellow flowers or a single flat-topped clusters at the top. Lance-shaped leaves are up to 5 in. (13 cm) long.

Habitat: Meadows, fields, pastures, open forests, stream banks.

Comments: An important nectar plant for bees, it blooms May–September.

LANTANA
Lantana spp.
Size: To 40 in. (1 m)

Description: Shrub has distinctive rounded clusters of 5-petaled flowers arranged in an inner and outer ring of differing colors. Opposite, heart-shaped leaves are toothed. Blooms throughout the year.

Habitat: Roadsides, waste areas, open woods.

Comments: The flowers may be orange, yellow, pink or white. Entire plant has a strong odor. Several native and introduced species are found in Texas. The native Texas lantana (*L. horrida*) is a favorite of hummingbirds.

CROSSVINE
Bignonia capreolata
Size: Vine to 50 ft. (15 m)

Description: Woody vine has showy, orange-red, tubular flowers that hang in clusters of 2–5. Flowers may be yellow with red throats, red with yellow throats or completely red. Opposite leaves are up to 6 in. (15 cm) long.

Habitat: Floodplains, uplands, hammocks.

Comments: Claws at the ends of the tendrils allow the plant to cling to stone, bricks and stucco without support. The name refers to the cross-shaped pattern that the stem reveals when cut. Blooms March–May.

COMMON SUNFLOWER
Helianthus annuus
Size: To 15 ft. (4.5 m)

Description: Tall, leafy plant with a hairy, branching stem supporting numerous, showy flowerheads with bright yellow rays and a dark-centered disk. Flowers are up to 5 in. (13 cm) across.

Habitat: Roadsides, disturbed areas, open fields.

Comments: The plant has been cultivated for centuries for its calorie-rich seeds. Blooms June–October.

CHOCOLATE DAISY
Berlandiera lyrata

Size: To 4 ft. (1.2 m)

Description: Velvety leaves have scalloped edges and are up to 6 in. (15 cm) long. Leafless stalk supports a flowerhead with 5-12 yellow rays surrounding a maroon central disk.

Habitat: Well-drained soils in grassy areas, roadsides, and plains in western Texas.

Comments: Plant has a chocolate aroma that is especially evident when plucking rays from the flowerhead. Also called chocolate flower, lyreleaf greeneyes, green-eyed lyre leaf, it blooms April–November.

GARDEN COREOPSIS
Coreopsis tinctoria

Size: To 4 ft. (1.2 m)

Description: Bright yellow daisy-like flowers are maroon near the central, red-purple central disk. Yellow petals have notched tips. Opposite leaves are divided into linear segments.

Habitat: Moist sandy soils on prairies, plains, meadows, pastures, roadsides.

Comments: Also known as plains coreopsis, golden tickseed, goldenwave, or calliopsis, it is cultivated extensively for its showy flowers. Native Americans used root tea to treat diarrhea and as an emetic. Blooms April–September.

AMERICAN LOTUS
Nelumbo lutea

Size: Flowers to 10 in. (25 cm) wide.

Description: Floating aquatic plant has fragrant, pale yellow flower. Large, bowl-shaped leaves often rise above the water and are up to 2 ft. (60 cm) wide. Fruits are nut-like kernels.

Habitat: Quiet streams, ponds, lakes, swamps.

Comments: Flowers open in the morning and close in late afternoon. The edible seed, when roasted, tastes like corn and is called "alligator corn". Blooms June–September.

RED & PINK FLOWERS

SCARLET GILIA
Ipomopsis rubra
Size: To 6 ft. (1.8 m)

Description: Stiff, unbranched, leafy stem supports a long, slender, branching cluster of showy, red, tubular flowers widely flaring at the rim. Flowers are marked with orange or yellow spots inside.

Habitat: Sandy and rocky soils in open areas, fields, open woodlands, riverbanks in central and east Texas.

Comments: Also called standing cypress, Texas plume, red Texas star, it blooms May–September. A favorite of hummingbirds.

SHOWY EVENING PRIMROSE
Oenothera speciosa
Size: To 2 ft. (60 cm)

Description: Slender, downy stems support nodding pink or white, cup-shaped, four-petaled flowers lined with pink or red veins. Flowers bloom in the evening and close each morning.

Habitat: Prairies, plains, roadsides.

Comments: Also called pink ladies and pink buttercups. Blooms February–July. Flowers and leaves are edible.

PHLOX
Phlox spp.
Size: 8–20 in. (20–50 cm)

Description: Sprawling herbs or small shrub with numerous showy, five-petaled, yellow-centered flowers. Flowers range in color from pink and lavender to yellow, violet, red and white. Narrow leaves are opposite.

Habitat: Dry soils in a variety of habitats.

Comments: There are 12 species and 19 subspecies of phlox found throughout Texas. They often form large colonies and are found in association with bluebonnet, blue-eyed grass and paintbrush.

OCOTILLO
Fouquieria splendens
Size: To 30 ft. (9 m)

Description: Gray, whip-like thorny branches fan out from the base. Small green leaves appear when there is adequate moisture, but drop off in times of drought. Bright red, tubular flowers bloom in tight, terminal clusters at stem tips.

Habitat: Sandy and rocky soils in desert flats and rocky slopes.

Comments: Flowers are an important nectar source for migrating hummingbirds. Also called devil's walking stick. Blooms March–August.

MEADOW PINK
Sabatia campestris
Size: To 20 in. (50 cm)

Description: Showy, 5-petaled, yellow centered pink flowers grow from the axils of upper leaves. Slender opposite leaves clasp the square stem.

Habitat: Dry or moist sandy soils in fields, pastures, prairies, woodland edges.

Comments: Often blooms in large colonies that create spectacular spring wildflower displays. Also called Texas star, rose gentian, prairie sabatia, it blooms April–July.

INDIAN PAINTBRUSH
Castilleja spp.
Size: To 3 ft. (90 cm)

Description: Ragged red wildflower often grows in dense colonies. Small green flowers are hidden at the base of showy bracts. Alternate leaves are hairy and up to 4 in. (10 cm) long.

Habitat: Woodlands, meadows, prairies, fields.

Comments: Related to snapdragons, paintbrushes occur in a variety of colors. Nine species are found in Texas, and many are often parasitic on the roots of other plants. Frequently planted along highways with bluebonnets and prickly poppy, it makes for spectacular spring wildflower displays. Blooms March–October.

BLAZINGSTAR
Liatris spp.

Size: To 5 ft. (1.5 m)

Description: Distinguished by its spike of feathery, red-purplish flowers with protruding styles. Alternate leaves grow crowded along stem length.

Habitat: Plains, prairies, hillsides, roadsides on gravelly and sandy soils.

Comments: Plant has many medicinal uses as a diuretic and a cure for laryngitis. Also called gayfeather, it blooms July–September.

CARDINAL FLOWER
Lobelia cardinalis

Size: 3–6 ft. (90–180 cm)

Description: Plant with spike of striking, red tubular flowers. Each flower has 3 spreading lower petals and 2 upper petals. Lower parts of the plant have lance-shaped leaves with toothed edges.

Habitat: Wet areas, along waterways, woodland edges, roadsides, meadows, pastures.

Comments: Also called scarlet lobelia, it is pollinated primarily by hummingbirds that are capable of reaching into the long, tubular flowers. Leaf teas were used for colds, fevers and headaches. Blooms May–December.

TURK'S CAP
Malvaviscus arboreus

Size: To 4 ft. (1.2 m)

Description: Erect or sprawling plant. Bright red, 5-petaled, hibiscus-like flowers have overlapping petals that form a loose tube with projecting stamens. Fruit is a small, edible apple.

Habitat: Well-drained soils on woodland edges, along streams, wooded slopes and ledges.

Comments: Named for the plant's resemblance to a Turkish fez. An important wildlife plant for hummingbirds, butterflies, moths, birds and mammals. Fruit is edible raw or cooked. Blooms May–November.

AMERICAN BASKET-FLOWER
Centaurea americana

Size: To 5 ft. (1.5 m)

Description: Stout, leafy, much-branched supports pink-lavender flowerheads with cream-colored centers that are up to 5 in. (13 cm) wide.

Habitat: Fields, prairies, pastures, waste areas, roadsides.

Comments: Common name refers to the stiff, straw-colored bracts beneath the flowerhead. Also called shaving brush and star thistle, it looks like a thistle but lacks any prickles. Blooms May–July.

WINECUP
Callirhoe involucrata

Size: To 3 ft. (90 cm)

Description: Sprawling, mat-forming plant has chalice-shaped, maroon, 5-petaled flowers with a white spot at the base.

Habitat: Sandy soils in open woods, scrublands, rocky hills, thickets.

Comments: Flowers open in the morning and close in the evening. Also called purple poppy mallow, it blooms March–June.

BLUE & PURPLE FLOWERS

TEXAS BLUEBONNET
Lupinus texensis

Size: To 18 in. (45 cm)

Description: Leafy plant has palmately-divided, velvety, star-shaped leaves. Blue, pea-shaped flowers bloom in a long terminal spike of up to 50 blossoms.

Habitat: Prairies, open fields, roadsides.

Comments: Also called Texas lupine, buffalo clover and wolf flower, it is widely planted throughout Texas along roadways. It attracts pollinators including bees and butterflies. Blooms March–May.

Texas' State Flower

PRAIRIE VERBENA
Glandularia bipinnatifida

Size: To 12 in. (30 cm)

Description: Hairy plant has square stems and opposite, highly-divided leaves that give the foliage a lacy appearance. Trumpet-shaped, pink, lavender or purple flowers bloom in rounded clusters

Habitat: Well-drained soils in open, grassy areas, woodland edges.

Comments: Also called Dakota vervain, Dakota mock vervain, moradilla and alfombrilla, it blooms throughout the year and is an important food source for butterflies.

ERYNGO
Eryngium leavenworthii

Size: To 40 in. (1 m)

Description: Prickly, thistle-like plant has deeply lobed leaves tipped with stiff spines. Flowerhead is a 2 in. (5 cm) tall purple cylinder sandwiched between spiny bracts that have a crown of spiny leaves. The entire plant turns from gray-green to purple in August.

Habitat: Gravelly, sandy, clay or limestone soils in prairies, plains and grassland.

Comments: Also called false purple thistle, it blooms July–October.

BLUE FLAG IRIS
Iris virginica

Size: To 3 ft. (90 cm)

Description: Narrow basal leaves often lie on the ground or in water. Showy, fragrant flowers have 3 petal-like sepals (splashed with yellow-orange) that droop downward and 3 inner sepals that are erect.

Habitat: Moist soils in meadows, swamps and along waterways.

Comments: Also called southern blue flag, it is found in northeast Texas and along the coastal plain. One of 5 species of blue flag native to Texas, it blooms April–May.

SPOTTED BEEBALM
Monarda punctata
Size: To 3 ft. (90 cm)
Description: Aromatic erect perennial has rosettes of yellowish, purple-spotted tubular flowers that grow in whorls. Each whorl is surrounded by large, conspicuous purplish leaf-like bracts. Flowers may also be white or green. Showy bracts may be pink, purple, white or yellow.
Habitat: Sandy soils in prairies, plains, meadows, pastures and fields.
Comments: Plant is irresistible to pollinators including butterflies and wasps. Plant contains essential oils that were historically used medicinally, for flavorings, perfumes and insect repellents. Blooms April–August.

PURPLE PASSIONFLOWER
Passiflora incarnata
Size: Climbing vine to 25 ft. (7.6 m) long
Description: Large lavender flowers to 3 in. (8 cm) wide have a striking fringe of thread-like petals and sepals. Leaves are up to 5 in. (13 cm) wide and have three lance-shaped leaflets. Fruit is an edible yellow-orange berry.
Habitat: Sandy soils in thickets, meadows, pastures, roadsides, woodland edges and along waterways.
Comments: Also called Maypop and apricot vine, it blooms April–September.

TAHOKA DAISY
Machaeranthera tanacetifolia
Size: To 16 in. (40 cm)
Description: Leaves are fern-like. Flowers have many thin purple rays surrounding a yellow central disk.
Habitat: Well-drained sandy or rocky soils in open areas on plains, meadows and deserts.
Comments: Plant often grows in clumps and mounds. Also called tansy-aster, it blooms May–October.

TEXAS BLUEBELL
Eustoma russellianum

Size: To 2 ft. (60 cm)

Description: Opposite blue-green leaves have wavy edges. Showy, cup-shaped flowers to 4 in. (10 cm) wide have 5-7 blue to blue-violet petals. A dark purple blotch surrounded by white is centered in the cup.

Habitat: Moist soils in prairies, fields, meadows, along waterways and ditches.

Comments: Also called showy prairie gentian, tulip gentian and lisianthus, it is a popular garden flower that has been overpicked from its native habitat in many areas and has been unable to naturally reseed. Blooms June–September.

BLUE-EYED GRASS
Sisyrinchium spp.

Size: To 2 ft. (60 cm)

Description: Slender stems support one or more delicate, 6-petaled, star-shaped flowers with a fine point at the petal tips. Flower color ranges from deep blue-violet to white, yellow, mauve and scarlet. Grass-like alternate leaves are up to 10 in. (25 cm) long.

Habitat: Moist, open areas in woodlands, meadows and mountains.

Comments: Related to popular ornamentals including freesias and gladiolas. Blooms April–September.

SPIDERWORT
Tradescantia spp.

Size: To 2 ft. (60 cm)

Description: Erect, branching stems support clusters of 3-petaled blue-violet to pinkish flowers that have 6 stamens with yellow anthers at their center. Arching, grass-like leaves are thought to resemble the splayed legs of a spider.

Habitat: Dry, sandy or fine soils in prairies, plains, meadows, pastures, open woodlands.

Comments: Flowers bloom only for one day. Also called spider lily, it blooms February–September.

TEXAS REGIONS

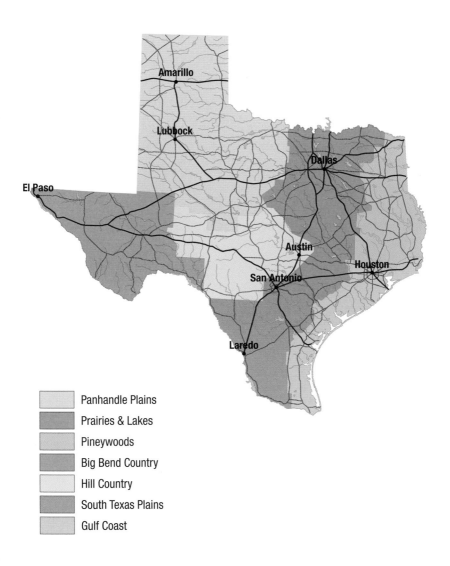

Panhandle Plains
Prairies & Lakes
Pineywoods
Big Bend Country
Hill Country
South Texas Plains
Gulf Coast

Texas can be divided into seven regions that generally reflect local ecosystems.

PANHANDLE PLAINS

The Panhandle Plains area includes the northernmost part of Texas and stretches downward to meet the Big Bend Country, Hill Country, and the Prairies and Lakes regions. The region is mostly flat, treeless grassland or plains. Some of the most well-known cities in this region are Amarillo, Brownwood, Canyon, and Lubbock.

PRAIRIES & LAKES

The Prairies and Lakes region is in north central and central Texas. It includes the Dallas/Fort Worth Metroplex, College Station (Texas A&M University) and Arlington (Six Flags, home stadiums for Dallas Cowboys and Texas Rangers). As the name implies, the area has lots of lakes.

PINEYWOODS

The easternmost region of Texas, down the Louisiana border to the Gulf Coast region, is the Pineywoods region. It is primarily a thick forest of pine trees, a woodland, which is part of a larger forest that extends into Louisiana, Arkansas, and Oklahoma. Swamps are common here, particularly in the southern most area of the region, which is called the "Big Thicket." Cities in the area are Conroe, Huntsville and Tyler.

BIG BEND COUNTRY

The Big Bend region is far west Texas, and it has wide-open spaces with rugged plateaus and desert mountains. The area offers the highest probability in Texas to view black bears and mountain lions. Named after the big bend of the Rio Grande River, there is also a national wildlife refuge and state park with the same name. Big Bend National Park is one of the most well-known national parks in the country. El Paso is the largest city in this region.

HILL COUNTRY

The Texas Hill Country is located pretty much in the center of the state. Its terrain is hilly, with many springs and steep canyons, and also hidden underground lakes and caves. The largest city in this region is the state capital, Austin.

SOUTH TEXAS PLAINS

The South Texas Plains region runs from the lower edge of the Hill Country and the western edge of the Gulf Coast region down into the subtropical regions along the Rio Grande River called the Lower Rio Grande Valley. Much of the region is dry and covered with grasses and thorny brush. However, the Lower Rio Grande Valley has a unique ecosystem and is home to palm trees, subtropical woodlands and lots of tropical birds. The largest city in this region is San Antonio, which is possibly the most popular vacation destination in the state of Texas.

GULF COAST

The Gulf Coast region stretches along the Gulf of Mexico for hundreds of miles, from the Mexican border to Louisiana. Near the gulf waters, you will find marshes, barrier islands, prairies, grasslands and bays. Some of the larger and most well-known cities in the Gulf Coast region are Houston, Galveston, Corpus Christi, and South Padre Island.

PANHANDLE PLAINS

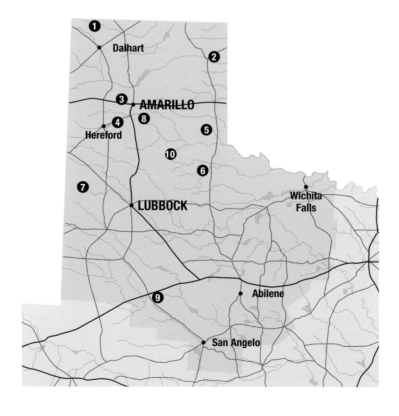

1 - RITA BLANCA NATIONAL GRASSLAND

On this national grassland, providing healthy feed for cattle appears to be the grassland's primary purpose. The Rita Blanca NG doesn't have outstanding recreational opportunities, but it is a special place. A place of endless grass rippling in the wind. A place where livestock and wildlife are fat and healthy. It is a place where visitors will find the "lone prairie" of song and folklore.

2 - GENE HOWE WILDLIFE MANAGEMENT AREA

The Gene Howe Wildlife Management Area (GHWMA) contains 5,886 acres of roughly two-thirds sandsage/midgrass rangeland and one third cottonwood/tallgrass bottomland. It is home to a trove of wildlife including game birds, deer, coyote, bobcat, jackrabbit, raccoon, eastern cottontail, black-tailed prairie dog, rabbits and rattlesnakes.

3 - AMARILLO BOTANICAL GARDENS

Dedicated to the art, science, and enjoyment of horticulture, these outdoor gardens feature displays on flora indigenous to the high plains region.

4 - BUFFALO LAKE WILDLIFE REFUGE

Buffalo Lake National Wildlife Refuge contains some of the best remaining short grass prairie in the United States, including 175 acres that have been designated a National Natural Landmark.

5 - PLAYA LAKES WILDLIFE MANAGEMENT AREA

The Playa Lakes Region is second only to the Gulf Coast in providing habitat for wintering waterfowl in the Central Flyway. The most conspicuous species during winter are Canada Geese and Snow Geese. Recent estimates suggest that 300,000 geese are found in the Playa Lakes Region.

6 - MATADOR WILDLIFE MANAGEMENT AREA

The 28,183-acre Matador Wildlife Management Area (MWMA) is located in the central Rolling Plains of Cottle County, Texas. Habitat types include mesquite uplands, shinnery oak rangeland and gravelly hills consisting of red berry juniper and mesquite mix, and bottomland.

7 - MULESHOE NATIONAL WILDLIFE REFUGE

One of the largest concentrations of lesser sandhill cranes in North America – often more than 100,000 birds at one time – winters at this grassland refuge. Thousands of ducks and geese use the refuge during the winter months.

8 - PALO DURO CANYON

Although the Panhandle region is known as the Panhandle Plains, these are actually high plains, complete with numerous deep canyons. The largest of these canyons is Palo Duro Canyon, known as the Grand Canyon of Texas.

9 - BIG SPRING STATE PARK

Howard County and Big Spring State Park are in an area where three ecological regions merge. To the north and east are the western Rolling Plains; to the south is the Edwards Plateau; and to the west are the Southern High Plains (also known as the Llano Estacado or the Staked Plains). The mixing of ecological regions results in a variety of plant and animal life.

10 - CAPROCK CANYON STATE PARK

Home to the state's official bison herd, there are numerous canyons that were once home to several different groups of Native Americans. The park also features a 120-acre lake, a prairie dog town and more than 100 miles of trails.

PRAIRIES & LAKES

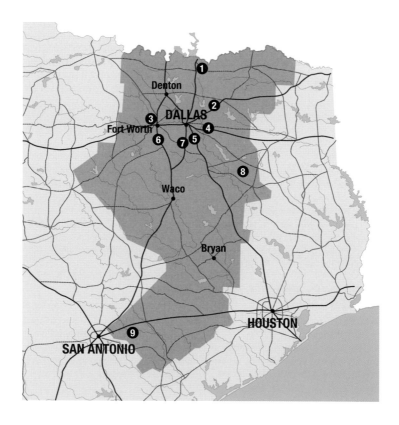

1 - HAGERMAN NATIONAL WILDLIFE REFUGE

Hagerman National Wildlife Refuge, a haven for migratory birds and other wildlife, lies on the Big Mineral Arm of Lake Texoma, on the Red River between Oklahoma and Texas. The refuge is made up of water, marsh and upland habitat, and visitors can hike, observe wildlife, hunt or fish throughout the year.

2- HEARD NATURAL SCIENCE MUSEUM & WILDLIFE SANCTUARY

The Heard Natural Science Museum & Wildlife Sanctuary emphasizes an appreciation of nature and its conservation through education. The emphasis of the Heard's education programs is children; however, the Heard also offers programs that will interest visitors of any age.

3 - FORT WORTH NATURE CENTER & REFUGE

The Fort Worth Nature Center & Refuge (FWNC&R) is a natural area comprised of forests, prairies and wetlands allowing you to step back in time and experience what the Fort Worth/Dallas Metroplex was like in the early 20th century.

4 - DALLAS ARBORETUM AND BOTANICAL GARDEN

The 66-acre Dallas Arboretum is one of the world's premier gardens and certainly one of the most colorful. Local residents have deemed this urban oasis to be the crown jewel of Dallas.

5 - PEROT MUSEUM OF NATURE & SCIENCE

The Perot Museum is a place where families can learn together, and individuals can take a break from their daily routines to explore the mysteries of science.

6 - FORT WORTH BOTANIC GARDEN

Enjoy all four seasons in the Fort Worth Botanic Garden. No matter the season there is always something spectacular to see. The most popular gardens are the Fuller, Rose and Japanese. Guests also enjoy the Native Texas Boardwalk, Rock Springs, Four Season and Back Yard Vegetable Garden. Mostly outside, but enclosed spaces as well. Huge grounds, formal and informal gardens, lots of roses and herbs. Over 90% of the Garden is free.

7 - TWELVE HILLS NATURE CENTER

The Nature Center has a beautiful entrance and gathering area as well as walking trails. A butterfly garden surrounds the entrance and includes many flowering native plants and shrubs. Twelve Hills proper has a trail around the edges of the five-acre nature center and returns to the entrance. There are many native wildflowers and trees in the mix. If you're observant, you'll see some of the wildlife that make their home here.

8 - EAST TEXAS ARBORETUM & BOTANICAL SOCIETY

One hundred acres of wooded beauty, trees, flowers and wildlife await your discovery at the East Texas Arboretum. The forest appears to come alive as you meander along two miles of woodland trails.

9 - PALMETTO STATE PARK

This unusual area resembles the tropics more than central Texas. Eastern and western species' ranges merge here. This results in an amazing diversity of plant and animal life.

PINEYWOODS

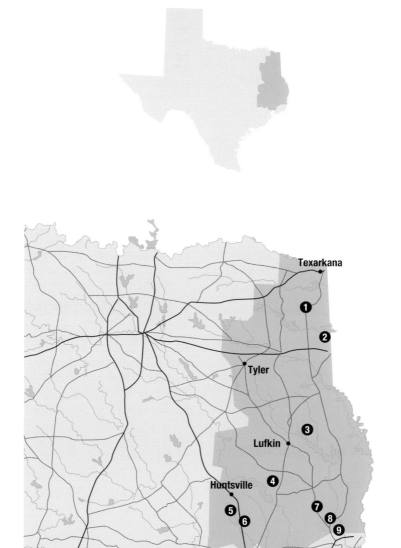

1 - ATLANTA STATE PARK

Atlanta State Park sits on the shores of Wright Patman Lake in the far northeast corner of Texas. Trees are the focal point at Atlanta State Park, with 90-foot tall pines and hardwoods studding the shores of Wright Patman Lake. Fall color is spectacular, while in the spring, dogwoods in bloom brighten the understory.

2 - CADDO LAKE STATE PARK AND WMA

Caddo Lake has an abundance of cypress trees, plant life and wildlife including 240 species of birds. Wildlife includes white-tailed deer, raccoons, beavers, minks, nutrias, squirrels, armadillos, frogs, turtles, snakes, alligators and a large variety of waterfowl.

3 - PINEYWOODS NATIVE PLANT CENTER

The Pineywoods Native Plant Center is a 42-acre garden on the north end of the Stephen F. Austin State University campus. It's a unique mixture of uplands, mesic mid-slopes and wet creek bottoms.

4 - ALABAMA CREEK WILDLIFE MANAGEMENT AREA

Alabama Creek's 14,561 acres are nestled in the Davy Crockett National Forest near the Neches River. Many people are drawn to this Pineywoods region of Texas in the early Spring (March) to witness the annual dogwood bloom.

5 - HUNTSVILLE STATE PARK

Huntsville State Park sits near the western edge of the southern pine belt. This area has mild, wet winters and hot, rainy summers. Nature lovers will find plenty to see here. Alligators, largemouth bass and crappie live in the lake. Around 250 species of birds have been identified in the park. During spring migration, many birds pass through the park. Wood warblers, thrushes and vireos are common in the park in late April and early May. In the summer, the forest is alive with the songs of breeding birds.

6 - BIG CREEK SCENIC AREA

For a chance to see many of the typical birds of the eastern Texas Pineywoods/Big Thicket region, take a short (or longer) hike along the trails at this beautiful 1,460-acre preserve of meandering creeks, lush pine-hardwood forest and varied flora and fauna.

7 - BIG THICKET NATIONAL PRESERVE

Life of all types abounds in the Big Thicket. This national preserve protects the incredible diversity of life found where multiple habitats converge in southeast Texas. Hiking trails and waterways meander through nine different ecosystems, from longleaf pine forests to cypress-lined bayous. It is a place of discovery, a place to wander and explore, a place to marvel at the richness of nature.

8 - ROY E. LARSON SANDYLAND SANCTUARY

This 5,600-acre ecologically diverse preserve is managed by The Nature Conservancy of Texas. Various forest and wetland communities intermingle in this part of the Big Thicket region. The sanctuary is part of a comprehensive effort to protect and restore the longleaf pine ecosystem on the West Gulf Coast.

9 - VILLAGE CREEK STATE PARK

Village Creek State Park teems with diverse plants and wildlife. Bottomland hardwood forests abound here. These wetlands provide habitat for beaver and river otter, as well as for many kinds of fish, snakes, turtles and frogs. Longleaf pine savannas, one of North America's rarest forest types, dominate the upper areas of the park providing perfect soils for post oak, yucca and prickly pear cactus.

BIG BEND COUNTRY

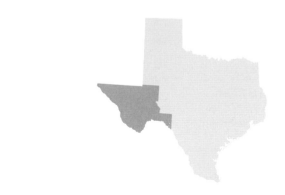

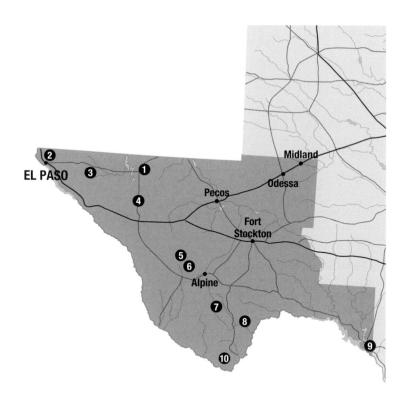

1 - GUADALUPE MOUNTAINS NATIONAL PARK

Guadalupe Mountains National Park protects the world's most extensive Permian fossil reef, the four highest peaks in Texas, an environmentally diverse collection of flora and fauna, and the stories of lives shaped through conflict, cooperation and survival.

2 - FRANKLIN MOUNTAINS STATE PARK

Although the park is completely within the city limits of El Paso, a robust and diverse ecosystem supports the many birds, reptiles and small mammals that live here. Over 100 species of birds visit or live here. Lechuguilla, sotol, ocotillo, several yuccas and numerous cacti grow in the park.

3 - HUECO TANKS STATE HISTORICAL PARK

For thousands of years, people have trekked to these rock hills in far west Texas. In earlier times, they came for the rainwater pooled in natural rock basins, or huecos ("whey-coes"). Visitors today marvel at the rock imagery left by those ancient people.

4 - SIERRA DIABLO WILDLIFE MANAGEMENT AREA

Area features a well-established mule deer population and free-ranging bighorn sheep. The rough, rugged terrain and steep canyons are surfaced by shallow, stony soils that support oak, juniper, mesquite, piñon, Douglas fir, aspen, maple, ponderosa pine and madrone.

5 - DAVIS MOUNTAINS STATE PARK

High in the mountains of west Texas you will find a beautiful and historic park. Javelinas are some of the most conspicuous wildlife residents of the park. The American Bird Conservancy has recognized the area as a Globally Important Bird Area. The park is home to over 260 species of birds and provides refuge to several species of concern.

6 - CHIHUAHUAN DESERT NATURE CENTER & BOTANICAL GARDEN

The Chihuahuan Desert Gardens (CDG) display the flora of the Chihuahuan Desert and adjacent regions in the United States and Mexico. The Gardens feature over 625 different species of plants, comprising one of the largest captive assemblages of Chihuahuan Desert flora in the world.

7 - ELEPHANT MOUNTAIN WILDLIFE MANAGEMENT AREA

Elephant Mountain WMA consists of 23,147 acres within the Trans-Pecos Ecological Region of west Texas. The large flat-topped mountain of igneous origin rises nearly 2,000 feet above the surrounding table land.

8 - BLACK GAP WILDLIFE MANAGEMENT AREA

Rugged wilderness, arid mountains and distinct wildlife characterize this wildlife management area, the largest in Texas. Tamaulipan desert scrub and Chihuahuan desert plant communities meet here contributing to the overall diversity. Wildlife includes 260 species of birds, bobcats, coyotes and a few black bear.

9 - AMISTAD NATIONAL RECREATION AREA

The Amistad area is a transition zone between eastern, western, northern and southern avifauna. Best known for excellent water-based recreation, camping, hiking, rock art viewing and its rich cultural history.

10 - BIG BEND NATIONAL PARK AND BIG BEND STATE PARK

Area features a solitary mountain range surrounded by weather-beaten desert. Tenacious cactus bloom in sublime southwestern sun, and diversity of species is the best in the country. The 800,000-acre national park contains three basic habitats: river, desert and mountains.

HILL COUNTRY

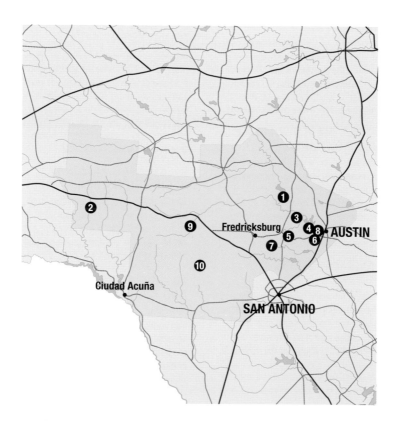

1 - INKS LAKE STATE PARK

This park sits on the east edge of the Llano Uplift, the geologic heart of Texas. It has some of the best views of pre-Cambrian (more than 600 million years old) geology in the state. The pink rock islands jutting up through the limestone in the park are metamorphic rock called Valley Spring gneiss ("nice"). Unique plants grow here and wildlife is abundant.

2 - CHANDLER INDEPENDENCE CREEK PRESERVE

The pristine waters of this desert oasis make a substantial contribution to the Peco River corridor wildlife community downstream. Furthermore, the creek itself sustains diverse and abundant flora and fauna including several rare and endangered species.

3 - HAMILTON POOL AND WESTCAVE PRESERVE

Hamilton Pool Preserve consists of 232 acres of protected natural habitat featuring a jade green pool into which a 50-foot waterfall flows. The area attracts birders from all over the world.

4 - TEXAS NATURAL SCIENCE CENTER

TNSC's world-renowned research has produced a collection of six million specimens in the disciplines of paleontology, geology, biology, herpetology, ichthyology and entomology. A working Paleontology Lab encourages visitors to interact with scientists preparing fossil finds.

5 - PEDERNALES FALLS STATE PARK

Here, the river drops about 50 feet in elevation over a distance of 3,000 feet. Water cascades over tilted, layered stair steps of limestone. Wildlife is abundant.

6 - ZILKER BOTANICAL GARDEN

Theme gardens such as the Rose, Herb and Japanese gardens are interconnected with streams, waterfalls and Koi-filled ponds. Its diverse topography is especially suited to depicting different habitats and displaying an array of native, hybrid and exotic plants.

7 - SOUTH LLANO STATE PARK

Area features a unique combination of rocky upland backcountry and a lush river bottom with a pecan grove. In October, monarch butterflies take shelter in the pecan branches at night as they journey south to Mexico. The park hosts one of the largest winter Rio Grande wild turkey roosts in central Texas.

8 - LADY BIRD JOHNSON WILDFLOWER CENTER

The Lady Bird Johnson Wildflower Center at The University of Texas at Austin is the state botanical garden and arboretum. The center features more than 900 species of native Texas plants in both garden and natural settings and is internationally recognized for its sustainable gardens, education and outreach programs and research projects.

9 - GUADALUPE RIVER STATE PARK

The Guadalupe River is the park's most out-standing natural feature with imposing bald cypress trees lining its banks. On a winding path through the park, the river courses over four natural rapids. Two steep limestone bluffs reflect the river's erosive power.

10 - LOST MAPLES STATE NATURAL AREA

Lost Maples holds steep and rugged limestone canyons, springs, plateau grasslands, wooded slopes and clear streams. The fall foliage of a large, isolated stand of uncommon Uvalde bigtooth maples is spectacular.

SOUTH TEXAS PLAINS

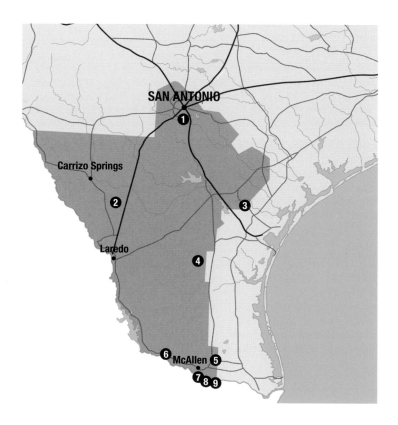

1 - SAN ANTONIO BOTANICAL GARDEN

With something always new to see at the San Antonio Botanical Garden, each season brings a variety of color and texture in the plant world. Visitors and Texas natives alike will enjoy the Texas Native Trail that showcases the diverse regions within the state.

2 - CHAPARRAL WMA

Chaparral Wildlife Management Area encompasses 15,200 acres of south Texas brush country in La Salle and Dimmit Counties approximately 100 miles southwest of San Antonio. The area is a haven for birds and four species on the Texas threatened list (Texas tortoise, the Texas horned lizard, the reticulated collared lizard and the Texas indigo snake).

3 - WELDER WILDLIFE REFUGE

The refuge is in the Tamaulipan province and is in a transition area between the tropics and the temperate zone. It, in fact, has a greater variety of plants and wildlife than any other area of comparable size in the world. More than 400 species and subspecies of birds have been observed in the refuge or its immediate vicinity.

4 - KING RANCH

King Ranch has a long history of wildlife management. As early as 1947, famed conservationist Aldo Leopold called King Ranch "one of the best jobs of wildlife restoration on the continent". Today, the ranch is a vital part of an incredibly diverse landscape in south Texas dubbed "The Last Great Habitat".

5 - VALLEY NATURE CENTER

The Valley Nature Center's 6-acre park is home to a wide variety of the Lower Rio Grande Valley's native plants and animals. The park is a wonderful natural oasis in the middle of the city.

6 - BENTSEN-RIO GRANDE VALLEY STATE PARK

This park is one of the most outstanding viewing areas in the country. It protects a part of the subtropical woodlands and shrublands that once covered much of the lower Rio Grande. Ocelot, jaguarundi, bobcat, coyote, javelina, Texas indigo snake, Texas tortoise and giant toad are viewable.

7 - SANTA ANA NATIONAL WILDLIFE REFUGE

Established in 1943 for the protection of migratory birds, Santa Ana National Wildlife Refuge is positioned along an east-west and north-south junction of two major migratory routes for many species of birds. It is the home of approximately 400 bird species, 450 types of plants and half of all butterfly species found in North America.

8 - RESACA DE LA PALMA STATE PARK

Abandoned coils of riverbed, known locally as resacas, are a magnet for wildlife when full. Resaca de la Palma is an especially rich birding environment. Colorful Neotropical and Nearctic migrants. The World Birding Visitor's Center is the portal to over eight miles of trails, four decks that overlook the four miles of resaca and a 2.76-mile tram loop that winds through the park.

9 - SABAL PALM GROVE SANCTUARY

For birders and nature-lovers, no visit to south Texas is complete without a stop at the Sanctuary. It is home to many native species of plants and animals that reach the northernmost limit of their Mexican range here and do not occur elsewhere in the U.S. Cradled in a bend of the Rio Grande along the U.S./Mexico border, the Sanctuary harbors one of the most beautiful and critical ecosystems of south Texas and Northern Mexico.

GULF COAST

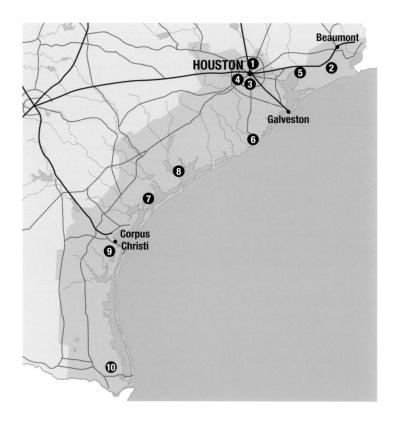

1 - JESSE H. JONES PARK & NATURE CENTER

Jesse H. Jones Park & Nature Center is a premier nature preserve that features a variety of plant and wildlife species inhabiting sandy beaches, swamps and sloughs with century-old cypress trees and a pristine floodplain located in a hardwood and pine forest.

2 - J.D. MURPHREE WMA

The J. D. Murphree WMA is a 24,498-acre tract of fresh, intermediate and brackish water, coastal marsh on the upper coast of Texas. The freshwater wetlands support an expanding association of exotic and noxious wetland plants as well as a vast diversity of wildlife.

3 - HOUSTON MUSEUM OF NATURAL SCIENCE

As one of the most heavily attended museums in the United States, it features a planetarium, a giant screen theater, nature center, butterfly center and a fascinating variety of permanent exhibit areas that examine astronomy, space, natural science, Texas wildlife and much more.

4 - HOUSTON ARBORETUM & NATURE CENTER

This 155-acre non-profit urban nature sanctuary provides education about the natural environment to people of all ages. It plays a vital role in protecting native plants and animals in the heart of the city where development threatens their survival.

5 - ANAHUAC NATIONAL WILDLIFE REFUGE

The meandering bayous of Anahuac National Wildlife Refuge cut through ancient flood plains, creating vast expanses of coastal marsh and prairie bordering Galveston Bay in southeast Texas. The marshes and prairies are host or home to an abundance of wildlife.

6 - BRAZORIA NATIONAL WILDLIFE REFUGE

Established to provide wintering habitat for migratory waterfowl and other bird species, the refuge serves as an end point for the ducks and geese migrating south along the Central Flyway for the winter. It also serves as an entry point for neotropical migratory songbirds headed north to their breeding grounds.

7 - ARANSAS NATIONAL WILDLIFE REFUGE

The mild winters, bay waters and abundant food supply attract more than 400 species of birds to the Aransas National Wildlife Refuge, including the whooping crane, one of North America's rarest birds. The refuge is surrounded by several shallow bays where the land shifts from salt to brackish and, eventually, freshwater marsh.

8 - MATAGORDA ISLAND

The Matagorda Island WMA consists of 56,688 acres of offshore barrier island and bayside marshes. The location and geological makeup of Matagorda Island, including coves, bays and marshes, provides a natural nursery for fish and shellfish. These crustaceans supply the shorebirds and wading birds with a plentiful food supply.

9 - SOUTH TEXAS BOTANICAL GARDENS & NATURE CENTER

Stunning floral exhibits and gardens are featured on winding trails through shaded native habitat, bridged ravines and natural wetlands.

10 - LAGUNA ATASCOSA NATIONAL WILDLIFE REFUGE

In a region of Texas some call the last great habitat, 97,000 acres of thorn forest intermingle with freshwater wetlands, coastal prairies, mudflats and beaches. The refuge is a premiere bird-watching destination with more recorded species of birds than any other refuge in the National Wildlife Refuge System.

MAMMALS

- [ ] American Badger
- [ ] American Beaver
- [ ] Atlantic Spotted Dolphin
- [ ] Axis Deer
- [ ] Barbary Sheep (Aoudad)
- [ ] Big Brown Bat
- [ ] Black Bear
- [ ] Black Rat
- [ ] Black-tailed Jackrabbit
- [ ] Black-tailed Prairie Dog
- [ ] Blackbuck
- [ ] Bobcat
- [ ] Bottlenosed Dolphin
- [ ] Cave Myotis
- [ ] Common Gray Fox
- [ ] Common Muskrat
- [ ] Common Porcupine
- [ ] Common Raccoon
- [ ] Coyote
- [ ] Desert Cottontail
- [ ] Desert Shrew
- [ ] Eastern Cottontail
- [ ] Eastern Gray Squirrel
- [ ] Eastern Mole
- [ ] Eastern Spotted Skunk
- [ ] Evening Bat
- [ ] Fallow Deer
- [ ] Fox Squirrel
- [ ] Hispid Cotton Rat
- [ ] Hoary Bat
- [ ] House Mouse
- [ ] Javelina
- [ ] Kit Fox
- [ ] Long-tailed Weasel
- [ ] Mexican Free-tailed Bat
- [ ] Mexican Ground Squirrel
- [ ] Mink
- [ ] Mountain Lion
- [ ] Mountain Sheep
- [ ] Nilgai (Blue Bull)
- [ ] Nine-banded Armadillo
- [ ] Northern River Otter
- [ ] Nutria
- [ ] Pronghorn
- [ ] Red Bat
- [ ] Red Fox
- [ ] Ringtail
- [ ] Rock Squirrel
- [ ] Sika Deer
- [ ] Southern Flying Squirrel
- [ ] Southern Plains Woodrat
- [ ] Spotted Ground Squirrel
- [ ] Striped Skunk
- [ ] Swamp Rabbit
- [ ] Texas Kangaroo Rat
- [ ] Texas Longhorn
- [ ] Texas Pocket Gopher
- [ ] Thirteen-lined Ground Squirrel
- [ ] Virginia Opossum
- [ ] White-footed Mouse
- [ ] White-tailed Deer
- [ ] Wild Hog

BIRDS

- [ ] American Avocet
- [ ] American Coot
- [ ] American Crow
- [ ] American Goldfinch
- [ ] American Kestrel
- [ ] American Oystercatcher
- [ ] American Robin
- [ ] American White Pelican
- [ ] American Wigeon
- [ ] Anhinga
- [ ] Bald Eagle
- [ ] Barn Swallow
- [ ] Barred Owl
- [ ] Belted Kingfisher
- [ ] Bewick's Wren
- [ ] Black Skimmer
- [ ] Black Vulture
- [ ] Black-bellied Whistling Duck
- [ ] Black-chinned Hummingbird
- [ ] Black-crested Titmouse
- [ ] Black-crowned Night Heron
- [ ] Black-necked Stilt
- [ ] Blue Jay
- [ ] Blue-gray Gnatcatcher
- [ ] Blue-winged Teal
- [ ] Brewer's Blackbird
- [ ] Brown Pelican

- [ ] Brown Thrasher
- [ ] Brown-headed Cowbird
- [ ] Burrowing Owl
- [ ] Canada Goose
- [ ] Carolina Chickadee
- [ ] Carolina Wren
- [ ] Cattle Egret
- [ ] Cedar Waxwing
- [ ] Chihuahuan Raven
- [ ] Chimney Swift
- [ ] Cliff Swallow
- [ ] Common Grackle
- [ ] Common Gallinule
- [ ] Common Yellowthroat
- [ ] Cooper's Hawk
- [ ] Crested Caracara
- [ ] Double-crested Cormorant
- [ ] Downy Woodpecker
- [ ] Eastern Bluebird
- [ ] Eastern Meadowlark
- [ ] Eastern Phoebe
- [ ] Eurasian Collared-dove
- [ ] European Starling
- [ ] Forster's Tern
- [ ] Golden-fronted Woodpecker
- [ ] Great Blue Heron
- [ ] Great Egret
- [ ] Great Horned Owl
- [ ] Great-tailed Grackle
- [ ] Greater Roadrunner
- [ ] Greater Yellowlegs
- [ ] Green Heron
- [ ] Green Jay
- [ ] Green-winged Teal
- [ ] Harris's Hawk
- [ ] Hermit Thrush
- [ ] House Finch
- [ ] House Sparrow
- [ ] Inca Dove
- [ ] Indigo Bunting
- [ ] Killdeer
- [ ] Ladder-backed Woodpecker
- [ ] Laughing Gull
- [ ] Lesser Goldfinch
- [ ] Lesser Yellowlegs
- [ ] Little Blue Heron
- [ ] Loggerhead Shrike
- [ ] Long-billed Curlew
- [ ] Mallard
- [ ] Monk Parakeet
- [ ] Mottled Duck
- [ ] Mourning Dove
- [ ] Neotropic Cormorant
- [ ] Northern Bobwhite
- [ ] Northern Cardinal
- [ ] Northern Flicker
- [ ] Northern Harrier
- [ ] Northern Mockingbird
- [ ] Northern Pintail
- [ ] Northern Shoveler
- [ ] Orange-crowned Warbler
- [ ] Orchard Oriole
- [ ] Osprey
- [ ] Painted Bunting
- [ ] Pied-billed Grebe
- [ ] Pileated Woodpecker
- [ ] Purple Martin
- [ ] Red-bellied Woodpecker
- [ ] Red-headed Woodpecker
- [ ] Red-shouldered Hawk
- [ ] Red-tailed Hawk
- [ ] Red-winged Blackbird
- [ ] Ring-billed Gull
- [ ] Ring-necked Pheasant
- [ ] Rock Pigeon
- [ ] Roseate Spoonbill
- [ ] Ruby-crowned Kinglet
- [ ] Ruby-throated Hummingbird
- [ ] Ruddy Duck
- [ ] Ruddy Turnstone
- [ ] Sanderling
- [ ] Sandhill Crane
- [ ] Scissor-tailed Flycatcher
- [ ] Sharp-shinned Hawk
- [ ] Snowy Egret
- [ ] Spotted Sandpiper
- [ ] Tricolored Heron
- [ ] Tufted Titmouse
- [ ] Turkey Vulture
- [ ] Verdin
- [ ] Vermillion Flycatcher
- [ ] White Ibis

- ☐ White-breasted Nuthatch
- ☐ White-crowned Sparrow
- ☐ White-eyed Vireo
- ☐ White-throated Sparrow
- ☐ White-winged Dove
- ☐ Wild Turkey
- ☐ Willet
- ☐ Wood Duck
- ☐ Wood Stork
- ☐ Woodhouse's Scrub Jay
- ☐ Yellow-bellied Sapsucker
- ☐ Yellow-billed Cuckoo
- ☐ Yellow-breasted Chat
- ☐ Yellow-crowned Night-Heron
- ☐ Yellow-rumped Warbler

REPTILES

- ☐ American Alligator
- ☐ Bull Snake
- ☐ Collared Lizard
- ☐ Copperhead
- ☐ Cottonmouth
- ☐ Desert Kingsnake
- ☐ Eastern Yellow-bellied Racer
- ☐ Great Plains Rat Snake
- ☐ Great Plains Skink
- ☐ Green Anole
- ☐ Kemp's Ridley Sea Turtle
- ☐ Mexican Milk Snake
- ☐ Oranate Box Turtle
- ☐ Red-eared Slider
- ☐ Slender Glass Lizard
- ☐ Smooth Softshell
- ☐ Snapping Turtle
- ☐ Texas Banded Gecko
- ☐ Texas Coral Snake
- ☐ Texas Diamondback Terrapin
- ☐ Texas Earless Lizard
- ☐ Texas Horned Lizard
- ☐ Texas Map Turtle
- ☐ Texas Rat Snake
- ☐ Texas River Cooter
- ☐ Texas Spiny Lizard
- ☐ Texas Tortoise
- ☐ Western Chicken Turtle
- ☐ Western Coachwhip

- ☐ Western Diamondback Rattlesnake
- ☐ Western Whiptail
- ☐ Yellow Mud Turtle

AMPHIBIANS

- ☐ Blanchard's Cricket Frog
- ☐ Bullfrog
- ☐ Eastern Newt
- ☐ Great Plains Narrowmouth Toad
- ☐ Green Toad
- ☐ Green Treefrog
- ☐ Gulf Coast Toad
- ☐ Smallmouth Salamander
- ☐ Southern Leopard Frog
- ☐ Texas Toad
- ☐ Tiger Salamander

FISHES

- ☐ Alligator Gar
- ☐ American Eel
- ☐ Atlantic Croaker
- ☐ Atlantic Stingray
- ☐ Black Crappie
- ☐ Black Drum
- ☐ Blue Catfish
- ☐ Blue Marlin
- ☐ Bluegill
- ☐ Bowfin
- ☐ Brown Trout
- ☐ Chain Pickerel
- ☐ Channel Catfish
- ☐ Cobia
- ☐ Common Carp
- ☐ Crevalle Jack
- ☐ Dolphinfish
- ☐ Flathead Catfish
- ☐ Florida Pompano
- ☐ Gafftopsail Catfish
- ☐ Gizzard Shad
- ☐ Grass Carp
- ☐ Greater Amberjack
- ☐ Green Sunfish
- ☐ Guadalupe Bass
- ☐ King Mackerel
- ☐ Lane Snapper
- ☐ Largemouth Bass

- ☐ Longear Sunfish
- ☐ Pinfish
- ☐ Rainbow Trout
- ☐ Red Snapper
- ☐ Redbreast Sunfish
- ☐ Redear Sunfish
- ☐ Redfish
- ☐ Sailfish
- ☐ Sheepshead
- ☐ Smallmouth Bass
- ☐ Snook
- ☐ Southern Flounder
- ☐ Speckled Trout
- ☐ Spotted Bass
- ☐ Spotted Gar
- ☐ Striped Bass
- ☐ Striped Mullet
- ☐ Tarpon
- ☐ Tripletail
- ☐ Warmouth
- ☐ White Bass
- ☐ White Crappie
- ☐ Wiper
- ☐ Yellow Bass

BUTTERFLIES & MOTHS

- ☐ American Lady
- ☐ American Snout
- ☐ American Tent Caterpillar Moth
- ☐ Black Swallowtail
- ☐ Black Witch
- ☐ Bordered Patch
- ☐ Buckeye
- ☐ Cabbage White
- ☐ Cecropia Moth
- ☐ Common Wood Nymph
- ☐ Eastern Tiger Swallowtail
- ☐ Giant Swallowtail
- ☐ Gray Hairstreak
- ☐ Great Purple Hairstreak
- ☐ Hackberry Emperor
- ☐ Imperial Moth
- ☐ Io Moth
- ☐ Julia
- ☐ Luna Moth
- ☐ Monarch

- ☐ Mourning Cloak
- ☐ Orange Sulphur
- ☐ Palamedes Swallowtail
- ☐ Pipevine Swallowtail
- ☐ Polyphemus Moth
- ☐ Queen
- ☐ Question Mark
- ☐ Red Admiral
- ☐ Red-spotted Purple
- ☐ Sachem
- ☐ Silver-spotted Skipper
- ☐ Sleepy Orange
- ☐ Southern Dogface
- ☐ Spicebush Swallowtail
- ☐ Spring Azure
- ☐ Tailed Blue
- ☐ Tawny Emperor
- ☐ Texan Crescent
- ☐ Variegated Fritillary
- ☐ Viceroy
- ☐ White-lined Sphinx
- ☐ Zebra Longwing

TREES & SHRUBS

- ☐ American Elm
- ☐ American Sycamore
- ☐ Baldcypress
- ☐ Black Cherry
- ☐ Black Walnut
- ☐ Black Willow
- ☐ Blackjack Oak
- ☐ Bur Oak
- ☐ Bush Palmetto
- ☐ Catclaw Acacia
- ☐ Cedar Elm
- ☐ Crapemyrtle
- ☐ Eastern Cottonwood
- ☐ Eastern Redbud
- ☐ Flowering Dogwood
- ☐ Honey Mesquite
- ☐ Juniper
- ☐ Live Oak
- ☐ Loblolly Pine
- ☐ Longleaf Pine
- ☐ Osage-orange
- ☐ Pecan

☐ Post Oak
☐ Red Maple
☐ Red Mulberry
☐ Shortleaf Pine
☐ Shumard Oak
☐ Southern Magnolia
☐ Sweetgum
☐ Texas Ash
☐ Texas Madrone
☐ Texas Persimmon
☐ Texas Sage
☐ Texas Sugarberry
☐ Wild Azalea
☐ Yaupon

☐ Spiderwort
☐ Spotted Beebalm
☐ Tahoka Daisy
☐ Texas Bluebell
☐ Texas Bluebonnet
☐ Turk's Cap
☐ White Dogstooth Violet
☐ White Prickly Poppy
☐ White Snakeroot
☐ Winecup
☐ Yucca

WILDFLOWERS

☐ American Basket-flower
☐ American Lotus
☐ Black-eyed Susan
☐ Blackfoot Daisy
☐ Blazingstar
☐ Blue Flag Iris
☐ Blue-eyed Grass
☐ Butterflyweed
☐ Cardinal Flower
☐ Chocolate Daisy
☐ Common Sunflower
☐ Coneflower
☐ Crimson-eyed Rose Mallow
☐ Crossvine
☐ Eryngo
☐ Garden Coreopsis
☐ Goldenrod
☐ Indian Blanket
☐ Indian Paintbrush
☐ Lantana
☐ Meadow Pink
☐ Morning Glory
☐ Ocotillo
☐ Phlox
☐ Prairie Verbena
☐ Prickly Pear Cactus
☐ Purple Passionflower
☐ Rain Lily
☐ Scarlet Gilia
☐ Showy Evening Primrose
☐ Spider Lily

Alternate
Spaced singly along the stem.

Anther
The part of the stamen that produces pollen.

Anadromous
Living in saltwater, breeding in freshwater.

Annual
A plant which completes its life cycle in one year.

Anterior
Pertaining to the front end.

Aquatic
Living in water.

Aquifer
Underground chamber or layer of rock that holds water.

Ascending
Rising or curving upward.

Barbel
An organ near the mouth of fish used to taste, touch, or smell.

Berry
A fruit formed from a single ovary which is fleshy or pulpy and contains one or many seeds.

Bloom
A whitish powdery or waxy covering.

Brackish
Water that is part freshwater and part saltwater.

Bract
A modified, often scale-like, leaf, usually small.

Branchlet
A twig from which leaves grow.

Boss
A rounded knob between the eyes of some toads.

Burrow
A tunnel excavated and inhabited by an animal.

Carnivorous
Feeding primarily on meat.

Catkin
A caterpillar-like drooping cluster of small flowers.

Cold-blooded
Refers to animals which are unable to regulate their own body temperature. 'Ectotherm' is the preferred term for this characteristic since many 'cold-blooded' species like reptiles are at times able to maintain a warmer body temperature than that of 'warm-blooded' species like mammals.

Conifer
A cone-bearing tree, usually evergreen.

Coral
The limestone skeletal deposits of coral polyps.

Coverts
Small feathers that cover the underside (undertail) or top (uppertail) of the base of bird's tail.

Deciduous
Shedding leaves annually.

Diurnal
Active primarily during the day.

Dorsal
Pertaining to the back or upper surface.

Ecology
The study of the relationships between organisms, and between organisms and their environment.

Endangered
Species threatened with extinction.

Epiphyte
A plant that obtains nourishment from nutrients in the air and rain. They often live on host plants like trees without harming them.

Endemic
Living only in a particular area.

Flower
Reproductive structure of a plant.

Flower stalk
The stem bearing the flowers.

Fruit
The matured, seed-bearing ovary.

Gamete
An egg or sperm cell.

Habitat
The physical area in which organisms live.

Herbivorous
Feeding primarily on vegetation.

Insectivorous
Feeding primarily on insects.

Introduced
Species brought by humans to an area outside its normal range.

Invertebrate
Animals lacking backbones, e.g., worms, slugs, crustaceans, insects, shellfish.

Larva
Immature forms of an animal which differ from the adult.

Lateral
Located away from the mid-line, at or near the sides.

Lobe
A projecting part of a leaf or flower, usually rounded.

Mesa
High, flat-topped mountain or hill with steeply sloping sides.

Molting
Loss of feathers, hair or skin while renewing plumage, coat or scales.

Morphs
A color variation of a species that is regular and not related to sex, age or season.

Nest
A structure built for shelter or insulation.

Nocturnal
Active primarily at night.

Omnivorous
Feeding on both animal and vegetable food.

Ovary
The female sex organ which is the site of egg production and maturation.

Perennial
A plant that lives for several years.

Petal
The colored outer parts of a flower head.

Phase
Coloration other than typical.

Pistil
The central organ of the flower which develops into a fruit.

Pollen
The tiny grains produced in the anthers which contain the male reproductive cells.

Posterior
Pertaining to the rear.

Sepal
The outer, usually green, leaf-like structures that protect the flower bud and are located at the base of an open flower.

Species
A group of interbreeding organisms which are reproductively isolated from other groups.

Speculum
A brightly colored, iridescent patch on the wings of some birds, especially ducks.

Spur
A pointed projection.

Subspecies
A relatively uniform, distinct portion of a species population.

Terrestrial
Land dwelling.

Threatened
Species not yet endangered but in imminent danger of being so.

Ungulate
An animal that has hooves.

Ventral
Pertaining to the under or lower surface.

Vertebrate
An animal possessing a backbone.

Warm-blooded
An animal which regulates its blood temperature internally. 'Endotherm' is the preferred term for this characteristic.

Whorl
A circle of leaves or flowers about a stem.

Woolly
Bearing long or matted hairs.

MAMMALS

Schmidly, D. J. and Bradley, R. D. *Mammals of Texas* – 7Th Edition. Austin: University of Texas Press. 2016.

Kavanagh, J. and Leung, R. *Texas Wildlife*. Tampa: Waterford Press. 2016.

Whitakcr, John O., Jr. *National Audubon Society Field Guide to North American Mammals*. Rev. ed. New York: Alfred A. Knopf, 1996.

Reid, F. A. *Mammals of North America*. Boston: Houghton Mifflin, 2006.

Kaufmann, K and Bowers, R. *Mammals of North America*. New York: Houghton Mifflin, 2007.

Murie, Olaus J. A Field Guide to *Animal Tracks*. New York: Houghton Mifflin, 1998.

Elbroch, Mark. *Mammal Tracks & Sign*. Mechanicsburg, PA: Stackpole Books. 2019.

Stokes, D. and Stokes, Lillian. *Stokes Guide to Animal Tracking and Behavior.* New York: Little Brown. 2018.

Farrand, John. Jr. *Familiar Animal Tracks*. New York: Alfred A Knopf. 1995.

BIRDS

Rappole, J. H. *Birds of Texas.* College Station: Texas A&M University Press. 1994.

Holt, H. *A Birder's Guide to the Texas Coast.* Colorado Springs: American Birding Association. 2017.

National Geographic Field Guide to Birds: Texas. Washington, D.C.: National Geographic Society, 2005.

Kavanagh, J. and Leung, R. *Birds of Texas.* Tampa: Waterford Press. 2017.

National Geographic Field Guide to the Birds of North America. 7th ed. Washington, D.C.: National Geographic Society, 2017.

Sibley, David Allen. *The Sibley Guide to Birds.* New York: Alfred A. Knopf, 2014.

Peterson, Roger Tory. *Peterson Field Guide to Birds of Texas.* Boston: Houghton Mifflin, 2012.

REPTILES & AMPHIBIANS

Dixon, J. R. *Amphibians and Reptiles of Texas.* College Station: Texas A&M University Press. 2013.

Kavanagh, J. and Leung, R. *Texas Reptiles and Amphibians.* Tampa: Waterford Press. 2019.

Behler, J. L. and King, W. F. *The Audubon Society Field Guide to North American Reptiles and Amphibians.* New York: Alfred A. Knopf, 1998.

Conant, R. and Powell, R. *Peterson Field Guide to Reptiles and Amphibians of Eastern and Central North America.* Boston: Houghton Mifflin, 2016.

FISHES

Thomas, C. and Bonner, T. H. *Freshwater Fishes of Texas – A Field Guide.* College Station: Texas A&M University Press, 2007.

Bosanko, D. *Saltwater Sport Fish of the Gulf Field Guide.* Cambridge: Adventure Publications, 2010.

Gilbert, Carter R. and James D. Williams. *National Audubon Society Field Guide to Fishes: North America.* Rev. ed. New York: Alfred A. Knopf, 2002.

Page, Lawrence and Brooks M. Burr. *A Field Guide to Freshwater Fishes: North America North of Mexico.* Boston: Houghton Mifflin, 1991.

BUTTERFLIES & MOTHS

Garrett, H. and Beck, M. *Texas Bug Book – The Good, the Bad and the Ugly.* Austin: University of Texas Press, 2005.

Weber, J. and Weber, L. *Native Host Plants for Texas Butterflies.* College Station: Texas A&M University Press, 2018.

Kavanagh, J. and Leung, R. *Texas Butterflies and Moths.* Tampa: Waterford Press. 2016.

Carter, David. *Eyewitness Handbooks: Butterflies and Moths.* New York: Dorling Kindersley, 1992.

BIBLIOGRAPHY

TREES

Tekiela, S. *Trees of Texas.* Cambridge: Adventure Publications, 2009.

Garrett, J. H. *Plants of the Metroplex.* Austin: University of Texas Press, 1998.

Kavanagh, J. and Leung, R. *Texas Trees and Wildflowers.* Tampa: Waterford Press. 2017.

Elias, Thomas S. *The Complete Trees of North America.* New York: Van Nostrand Reinhold, 1987.

Little, Elbert L. *National Audubon Society Field Guide to North American Trees: Eastern Region.* New York: Alfred A. Knopf, 1980.

WILDFLOWERS

Eason, M. *Wildflowers of Texas.* Portland: Timber Press, 2018.

Ajilvsgi, G. *Wildflowers of Texas.* Fredricksburg: Shearer Publishing, 2003.

Niering, W. A. and Thierer, J. W. *The Audubon Society Field Guide to North American Wildflowers – Eastern Region.* New York: Alfred A. Knopf, 2001.

Venning, D. *Wildflowers of North America.* New York: Golden Press, 1984.

NATURAL HISTORY

Chapman, B. R. and Bolen, E. G. *The Natural History of Texas.* College Station: Texas A&M University Press. 2018.

Parker, M. O. and Parker, J. *Explore Texas – A Nature Travel Guide.* College Station: Texas A&M University Press. 2016.

White, M. *Exploring the Great Texas Coastal Birding Trail.* Helena: Falcon Press. 2004.

Graham, G. L. *Texas Wildlife Viewing Guide.* Helena: Falcon Press. 1992.

Wauer, R. H. and Fleming, C. M. *Naturalist's Big Bend.* College Station: Texas A&M University Press. 2001.

WEB SOURCES

Texas Parks & Wildlife Department – tpwd.state.tx.us

Mammals – http://www.nsrl.ttu.edu/tmot1

Birds – http://tx.audubon.org/birds

Reptiles and Amphibians – www.herpsofTexas.org

Fishes – www.fishesofTexas.org
        Txstate.fishesoftexas.org

Insects – Texas A&M – http://texashighplainsinsects.net/

USDA Plants Database – plants.usda.gov/about_plants.html

Natural History of Texas – Texas Memorial Museum - tmm.utexas.edu

Natural Attractions – TourTexas.com